MW01193478

THE UNITED STATES, CHINA, AND THE COMPETITION FOR CONTROL

This book considers whether the United States and the People's Republic of China have irreconcilable visions of world order.

The United States, China, and the Competition for Control evaluates the twin claims that China seeks to dismantle the post–World War II international order and that the United States seeks to defend it. It defines the post–war order and examines how the United States and China have behaved within and in relation to it since 1945. An analysis of the two states' rhetoric and policy reveals that their preferences for international order are not as divergent as today's conventional wisdom suggests. The book therefore concludes that U.S. policies that treat China as a threat to international order are misplaced and offers policy recommendations for how the United States can both preserve the post–war order and protect its vital national interests.

The book will be of interest to foreign policy practitioners, commentators, and analysts, as well as students and scholars of security studies, international relations, and geopolitics.

Melanie W. Sisson is a fellow in the Foreign Policy program's Strobe Talbott Center for Security, Strategy, and Technology at the Brookings Institution, USA. She researches the use of the armed forces in international politics, U.S. national security strategy, and defense applications of emerging technologies. Sisson earned a doctorate in political science from the University of Colorado at Boulder and a master's from the Columbia University School of International Affairs. She is co-editor of *Military Coercion and US Foreign Policy: The Use of Force Short of War* (Routledge, 2020).

Routledge Studies in US Foreign Policy

Series Editors

Inderjeet Parmar
City University
John Dumbrell
Durham University

This new series sets out to publish high-quality works by leading and emerging scholars critically engaging with United States Foreign Policy. The series welcomes a variety of approaches to the subject and draws on scholarship from international relations, security studies, international political economy, foreign policy analysis and contemporary international history.

Subjects covered include the role of administrations and institutions, the media, think tanks, ideologues and intellectuals, elites, transnational corporations, public opinion, and pressure groups in shaping foreign policy, US relations with individual nations, with global regions and global institutions and America's evolving strategic and military policies.

The series aims to provide a range of books—from individual research monographs and edited collections to textbooks and supplemental reading for scholars, researchers, policy analysts and students.

Nineteenth Century America in the Society of States
Reluctant Power
Edited by Cornelia Navari and Yannis A. Stivachtis

The Sources of Great Power Competition
Rising Powers, Grand Strategy, and System Dynamics
Edited by J. Patrick Rhamey Jr. and Spencer D. Bakich

The United States, China, and the Competition for Control
Melanie W. Sisson

For more information about this series, please visit: https://www.routledge.com/Routledge-Studies-in-US-Foreign-Policy/book-series/RSUSFP

THE UNITED STATES, CHINA, AND THE COMPETITION FOR CONTROL

Melanie W. Sisson

Routledge
Taylor & Francis Group

LONDON AND NEW YORK

Designed cover image: © Gwengoat—Getty Images

First published 2025
by Routledge
4 Park Square, Milton Park, Abingdon, Oxon OX14 4RN

and by Routledge
605 Third Avenue, New York, NY 10158

Routledge is an imprint of the Taylor & Francis Group, an informa business

© 2025 Melanie W. Sisson

The right of Melanie W. Sisson to be identified as author of this work has been asserted in accordance with sections 77 and 78 of the Copyright, Designs and Patents Act 1988.

British Library Cataloguing-in-Publication Data
A catalogue record for this book is available from the British Library

Library of Congress Cataloging-in-Publication Data
Names: Sisson, Melanie, author.
Title: The United States, China, and the competition for control / Melanie W. Sisson.
Description: Abingdon, Oxon ; New York, NY : Routledge, 2025. | Series: Routledge studies in US foreign policy | Includes bibliographical references and index.
Identifiers: LCCN 2024025522 (print) | LCCN 2024025523 (ebook) | ISBN 9781032703527 (hardback) | ISBN 9781032723341 (paperback) | ISBN 9781032723358 (ebook)
Subjects: LCSH: Great powers. | Government competition—United States. | Government competition—China. | Security, International—United States. | Security, International—China. | United States—Foreign relations—China. | China—Foreign relations—United States
Classification: LCC JZ1310 .S57 2025 (print) | LCC JZ1310 (ebook) | DDC 327.73051—dc23/eng/20240802
LC record available at https://lccn.loc.gov/2024025522
LC ebook record available at https://lccn.loc.gov/2024025523

ISBN: 978-1-032-70352-7 (hbk)
ISBN: 978-1-032-72334-1 (pbk)
ISBN: 978-1-032-72335-8 (ebk)

DOI: 10.4324/9781032723358

Typeset in Sabon
by Apex CoVantage, LLC

CONTENTS

1

INTRODUCTION

* * *

It has too readily been accepted that the United States is the standard-bearer of a defense-oriented, non-interventionist, rules-based international order, and too little questioned that the People's Republic of China (PRC) seeks to break that order and supplant it with a malign system that is rent-seeking, encouraging of internal repression, and tolerant of external aggression—one that "only works for [the PRC] but not for the rest of us".[1] China's system of internal governance inarguably is incompatible with the values that animate the system of governance of the United States and the world's other liberal democracies. There also is no question that under the leadership of Xi Jinping, China has behaved in ways that break with a number of established international practices, and in some cases, that challenge U.S. interests.[2] Yet it is an overextension to conclude that this means China's preferences for the conduct of international affairs—for international order—are definitionally antithetical to those of the United States and other liberal democracies. On this, the conviction has preceded the evidence.

Review of the post–World War II period in fact serves to de-romanticize the relationship the United States has had with the order it helped to create. The United States sometimes has emphasized and firmly upheld the importance of post-war principles and institutions and, at other times, has ignored them entirely. These contradictions are not surprising—the job of policymakers is to set priorities and make tradeoffs among competing interests and imperatives—but they should not be dismissed or sanitized. They certainly are not as readily overlooked, or as quickly forgiven, by large swathes of the international community.[3]

More important than the fidelity with which the United States depicts its past performance, however, is the extent to which America's current

DOI: 10.4324/9781032723358-1

strategy for competing with China trends more toward degrading than it does toward defending the post–war order. Despite its rhetoric, the reality is that U.S. foreign policy is flirting with abandoning the post–war order's institutions and rejecting its core principles. If one takes U.S. policymakers at their word, then this retrenchment is caused by the belief that non-liberal economic policies and growing reliance on the threat of force are necessary to defend the order against China's authoritarian designs—that the post–war order, in other words, must be burned to be saved. It is for historians to determine whether this sentiment reflects a congenital anxiety that the nation's own democracy cannot withstand the pressures of an order in which non-democracies are too powerful or too numerous, or simply the desire for America to remain the world's dominant state.[4]

A review of the record also produces a rather encouraging picture of China's regard for and treatment of the principles and institutions that have given substance and structure to international politics since the end of World War II, in the past and the present. It reveals a China that most experts judge to be neither ideologically nor territorially expansionist and to be far more interested in revising the rules of the post-war institutions than in eliminating them. In many cases, the changes China seeks to make to those rules reflect the Chinese Communist Party's (CCP) long-standing and intense defensiveness against what it regards as intrusions into China's domestic affairs and the Party's exercise of sovereignty. This defensiveness is not unique to, but is especially visible in, Beijing's reactions to efforts to elevate the role of human rights in international relations, most especially during the post–Cold War period. Although this is an area of clear divergence with the United States and other liberal democracies, it is not a new feature of Chinese policy, nor is it an indicator of an ambition to rewire the whole of international order.

China's preferred international order does, however, differ in one important respect from the one it inhabits today. The post–war order was built on the foundation of U.S. military power, and it continues to operate on the presumption of the presence and potential application of that power. The U.S. military largely underwrites the flow of goods across the world's oceans, its overseas posture is a check on the worst impulses of the world's most volatile actors, and its alliances moderate regional insecurities and suppress urges toward arms racing and nuclearization. China wishes for the role of the United States in East Asia, and the military presence that anchors it, to diminish and for its own role to grow. This would make Beijing feel more secure and endow it with greater latitude to pursue its own regional interests—inclusive of trade relationships, claims on maritime spaces, and unification with the self-governing island of Taiwan, on its own terms. It also would provide China with greater stature, and leverage, in international affairs more broadly.

This desire to push the United States out of its neighborhood is a natural outcome of China's growing economic and military stature; it is what aspiring, and actual, great powers tend to do. It also is an enduring source of risk in the bilateral relationship, as China continues to seek ways in which to make it ever more uncomfortable for the United States to operate there, and as the United States continues to seek ways in which to make it ever more clear that it is not leaving. This conflict of interest is serious and increasingly dangerous, and it will require careful handling by both the United States and China into the indefinite future. It does not, however, mean that China is seeking to break, or even simply to opt out of, the post–war order in whole. Nor does it mean that it is impossible for the two powers to achieve a stable regional status quo.

China is far from insensitive to the benefits it enjoys from being part of a functioning global system and, by its own account, recognizes that it has not yet ascended to great power status, much less achieved the global reach exercised by the United States. The challenge U.S. policy-makers are facing today thus is not that "the PRC is the only competitor with both the intent to reshape the international order and, increasingly, the economic, diplomatic, military, and technological power to advance that objective".[5] What U.S. policymakers are instead confronting is that China's success in demonstrating that its illiberal political system is socially stable, economically productive, and militarily capable will make it harder for the United States to pursue its own goals and interests, whether inside or outside the structures of this post-war, or of any other, international order. China's rise, in other words, positions it to be increasingly able to resist U.S. preferences for itself and on behalf of others, if it so chooses.[6]

For now, China seems more inclined to do so within the structures of the post–war order than without it—to seek to make its own interpretation of the order's principles more prominent, and its influence more present in the rule-making processes and outputs of the order's institutions. If the United States also wishes to retain the post–war order and wishes for the order's principles and institutions to hew more toward U.S. interests and values than toward China's, then it will need to work actively and effectively within them to make it so. It also will need to retain the credibility of its readiness to apply military force in defense of its own and of its allies' territorial integrity and to protect freedom of transit under, on, over, and through the world's seas and skies. This is why, if it persists into the future, the nationalist sentiment embodied in President Donald J. Trump's repeated threats to withdraw the United States from its long-standing alliance structure in Europe and his suggestions of the same in East Asia will do more to undermine the international order than any policy devised by the CCP.[7]

The narrative that the United States seeks to defend and that China seeks to degrade the post–war order nonetheless is being used to justify economic protectionism, as leverage in trade relationships with current and potential partners and as the rationale for expanding U.S. defense commitments and military posture in the Indo-Pacific. These policies are straining U.S. relationships globally, and states wishing to have productive relations with both the United States and China worry they soon will find that possibility foreclosed.[8] So too is the U.S. approach to the "China challenge" shrinking the space available for bilateral exchange and cooperation and exacerbating mild irritants, persistent tensions, and longstanding disagreements. These outcomes are counter to U.S. national interests and to global peace and security. As such, they also are reminders that it will not be sufficient, and might be counterproductive, to treat defense of vital U.S. interests as lesser included cases of defense of the post–war order.

Although not a certainty, most reputable projections agree that China is more likely than not to continue on its journey to becoming an established, modern great power. A U.S. strategy for competing with China that treats this rise as a threat to the international order might prove successful. It also might not, and it carries costs and risks in the trying— among them the possibility of global economic dislocation and war. The alternative is for U.S. policymakers to seek to defend U.S. national interests by staying true to the post–World War II order's pragmatic intent: to prevent that war's recurrence by making it less likely that economic and ideological disagreements will cause the world's major powers to stumble into, or to choose, conflagration.

This purpose is becoming obscured in U.S. discourse, increasingly overwritten by a narrative that makes order the object of great power conflict, not the means of managing it. It is a dangerous inversion, one that converts negotiating the rules of international affairs into a competition to set them. It elevates the importance of every disagreement and inflates the implications of their outcomes. The result is a U.S. foreign policy that is defensive and Newtonian—seeking to match each of China's diplomatic, economic, and military actions with an equal and opposite reaction of its own. It is a reflex that too often loses sight of the objectives of the post–war order and that presumes policy has more control over events than it often does.

Which Order?

When policymakers and commentators in the United States describe the international order, it usually is in terms of the combination of institutions, alliances, rules, and norms that have evolved to characterize international politics in the period after World War II.[9] The post-war institutions are depicted as central to this order and as intentionally liberalizing in orientation, designed by American and British post-war planners as essential ingredients of a larger project to achieve peace by increasing global wealth, protecting human rights, and progressively converting the internal politics of other states to democracy. So too does the dominant narrative unfailingly position the United States as the primary promoter and defender of the post–war order and of its liberalizing mission.

This depiction of the post–war order and interpretation of its intent is half right and half wrong. The post–war order was conceived as a means through which to try to achieve great power peace—but the strategy was not global wealth and internal political liberalization. The order was instead conceived more modestly, as a means through which to control national-level interests and fears that, having twice been left unmanaged, twice had produced the worst possible outcome.

To achieve this, the goal was to address what were believed to have been root causes of the world wars: protectionist and discriminatory economic policies that came at the expense of others, and the absence of impediments to the use of force.[10] If global economic growth and the spread of internal political liberalization were to follow from the operation of the order, it would be a welcome effect. But that pursuit was not primary to the objectives of generating economic growth within those democracies that already existed and of preventing wars of aggression against them.

Similarly, most of the norms and patterns of behavior that many today associate with the post–war order are not products of its founders' design but of America's power. This is especially the case for the set of expectations concerning state regard for human rights. The Genocide Conventions (1948) prohibiting the intentional eradication of a "national, ethnic, racial or religious group, in whole or in part", and the Geneva Conventions (1949), which place limits on state behavior during times of war, are binding treaties but they are not part of the U.N. Charter.[11] The more broadly conceived 1948 Universal Declaration of Human Rights (1948), which captures bodily integrity, self-determination, and political and religious liberty, is neither part of the U.N. Charter nor a binding treaty. Protection and advancement of these rights did not become a prominent feature of U.S. foreign policy until the administration of President Jimmy Carter in the mid-1970s, in part as a reaction to the war in Vietnam and to revelations about U.S. interventions (many of them covert) in Latin America, the Middle East, Southeast Asia, and Africa. The idea that states have an obligation not only to not commit genocide themselves but also to act to stop others from doing so—the "responsibility to protect"—emerged in the early 2000s, and norms about reproductive rights, sexual orientation, and gender identity have emerged even more recently than that.

Noting this progression is not to be dismissive of America's past investments in generating these and other norms and of seeking to establish their role in international politics, but it is important to distinguish between elements that are constitutive of the post–war order and those that are artifacts of it. Norms are the latter: there are no clear inclusion criteria to distinguish norms that are part of the post–war order from those that are not, and there are no widely accepted cut-points or thresholds for how many of them, or which among them, are necessary or sufficient to create and uphold it. The converse also is true: there is no shared understanding of how many of today's norms if degraded, or of which specific norms among them if lost, would undo the post–war order entirely. Norms thus are most tractably understood as patterns of behavior that express a preference—one's own, or a concession to someone else's—for doing things one way rather than another.

China's growing power makes it possible to imagine an international order, whether this one, or a different one, that privileges America's liberal preferences less and China's illiberal preferences more. Indeed, China's efforts to shift that balance are increasingly visible—in its activism in international digital standards-setting organizations, for example, and in its coercive approach to promoting its territorial, jurisdictional, and sovereignty claims. These and other diplomatic, economic, and military activities short of war that subvert practices endorsed by the United States and its allies and partners are designed to ask, "Who cares about this particular norm enough to enforce it, and at what cost?" China's use of such tactics to pursue discrete policy objectives, to be "selectively revisionist", is therefore rightfully cause for concern. It also should be expected to continue until the United States and its allies and partners begin to demonstrate a collective seriousness of purpose in answering these questions with firmness and alacrity.[12] These behaviors, however, do not themselves constitute a major break with the principles and institutions of the post–war order and should not be the basis for extrapolation about China's ambitions to create a new one.

The China Challenge

The conclusion that China's domestic illiberalism and its dissatisfaction with regional and other norms reflect preferences that are incompatible with the post–war order comes from somewhere. These behaviors, interpretations of Chinese strategy documents and CCP pronouncements, and theories of international relations can be, and often are, combined to make a compelling case.

Much of that case rests on two mutually reinforcing, and fairly widely accepted, propositions. The first is that there has been a transition in Chinese foreign policy since the end of the Cold War from a focus on establishing its own place as a great power in the global order to seeking actively to displace and, ultimately, to replace the United States as the world's most influential, indeed the world's dominant, actor. As explained by one academic and government official:

> Xi's ambition is to reorder the world order. . . . The path to achieving this vision is a difficult one. It requires challenging both the position of the United States as the world's dominant power and the international understandings and institutions that have been in place since the end of World War II.[13]

The second proposition is that China is seeking to do so by establishing an illiberal hegemony first regionally, and then globally, largely through the development and application of military capability:

> An aspirant like China cannot expect to establish regional hegemony with inducements and political and economic coercion alone . . . nothing is more effective leverage than the threat of physical violence. . . . Unsurprisingly, the growth of China's military maps very closely to this logic. Beijing has developed armed forces that are highly suited to attacking nearby states while being able to strike effectively at more distant potential coalition members, including the United States.[14]

China's growth as a military power thus is considered worrisome "not only because of the near-term risk of conflict over Taiwan, but also because it raises fundamental questions about America's role in the region and the world".[15]

A particularly influential argument is based on an analysis of archival and contemporary CCP materials.[16] The key portions of the texts from which the author derives conclusions about China's ambitions, however, are subject to interpretations other than that arrived at by the author—it is possible, that is, to read the materials presented and disagree with the conclusion that China seeks to displace the United States as the "world's leading state". One of the exchanges featured to make this case, for example, can be read in at least two ways. One is as an acknowledgment that China might have an ambition to replace the United States and to create a different world order. Another is as an acknowledgment that China's ambitions might be lesser:

> Lee Kuan Yew—the visionary politician who built modern Singapore and personally knew China's top leaders—was asked by an interviewer, "Are Chinese leaders serious about displacing the United States as the number one power in Asia and in the world?" He answered with an emphatic yes. "Of course. Why not?" he began, "They have transformed a poor society by an economic miracle to become now the second-largest economy in the world" . . . China, he continued, boasts "a culture 4,000 years old with 1.3 billion people, with a huge and very talented pool to draw from. How could they not aspire to be number one in Asia, and in time the world? . . . every Chinese wants a strong and rich China, a nation as prosperous, advanced, and technologically competent as America, Europe, and Japan . . . China wants to be China and accepted as such, not as an honorary member of the West". China might want to "share this century" with the United States, perhaps as "co-equals", he noted, but certainly not as subordinates.[17]

A focus on the first clause "How could they not aspire to be number one in Asia, and in time the world?", rather than on the second, "China might want to 'share this century' with the United States, perhaps as 'co-equals' . . . but certainly not as subordinates", colors the remainder of the analysis, both its depiction of China's goals and its strategy to achieve them. Absent that framing, however, the passages from Chinese assessments of "great changes unseen in a century"—U.S. decline, China's rise, and the opportunities this presents for China—can easily be read as sober analysis, even if one disagrees with the conclusions reached. Many of the quotations offered as textual evidence from official CCP statements, including from Xi Jinping's own speeches and from the writings of Chinese thinkers, seem fairly observational and, if not unassuming, then at least far from impatient or rapacious: "U.S. withdrawal has led to greater confidence in and respect for China's role, enabling China to move closer to the center of the world stage through participating in global governance and expanding its clout and voice in the world"; "the greatest change of the 'changes unseen in a century' is precisely *China's rise* (op cit) . . . which fundamentally changes the international power balance";

> [f]or China, the great changes bring both challenges and opportunities. The challenge mainly comes from the strategic game of great powers. The United States has regarded China as a strategic competitor, and the overall strength of the United States is still stronger than that of China. In this case, whether it can cope with the strategic competitive pressure of the United States is a severe test for China.[18]

Yet the author's interpretation of these and other writings is that they reflect a consensus within China that it needs "an approach integrating political, economic, and military means to achieve [its] lofty goals and displace the United States from global order".[19] It is, of course, possible that this interpretation is correct. Yet even these and other quotations selected to make this case do not, on a prima facie basis, consistently portray China's desire for rejuvenation as a goal that requires surpassing the United States in global leadership or provide statements of intent to replace the post–war order with one that is China-centric.

The case that China's grand strategy—its management of its economic and foreign policies (diplomatic and military) for purposes of promoting China's prosperity and security—has changed, however, is convincing. There is a clear progression from "hiding and biding", the phrase past Chinese leaders used to describe a "conscious strategy of non-assertiveness", to the current day's focus on taking advantage, through action, of the "great changes unseen in a century".[20] And there is no question that China's strategy now includes challenging some of the international norms and practices that have developed in the 70 years since the end of World War II. This is especially true in its own region, where exerting its influence inevitably bumps up against U.S. efforts to maintain its own. This fact, however, does not demonstrate an intent to disassemble the post–war order. Neither does China's desire to be "a leading country in comprehensive national strength and international influence", and to continue its movement "closer toward the world's center stage", eliminate the possibility that it might be willing to occupy that center, in the words of Lee Kuan Yew, as co-equals with the United States. Indeed, in a 2023 face-to-face meeting, President Xi Jinping is reported to have expressed to President Joe Biden that "The world is big enough to accommodate both countries, and one country's success is an opportunity for the other".[21]

The second proposition, that China is growing its military power for purposes of imposing a regional hegemony on its way to achieving a global one, is largely based on one body of Western theories of international relations. These theories are part of the realist paradigm, which argues that all states seek security through the accumulation of military advantage relative to neighbors nearby and relative to those farther afield. One particular strand of realist theory, called the power transition theory, predicts conflict when the distribution of power among leading states shifts, as the declining state's desire to retain its power advantage becomes irreconcilable with the rising state's determination to reverse it. Those convinced by power transition theory thus see China as a threat regardless of whether the U.S. policy response to its growth is moderate or aggressive.[22] These and other predictions from realism, however, were developed largely from the study of Western European history, and it is worth considering that they may not be so generalizable as to negate China's own historical experience and traditions of thought. Even if they are, moreover, the dynamics these theories describe are not laws of nature, impervious to human agency.

Evaluating the Record

Just as it is possible and necessary to question China's intentions toward the post–war order, moreover, so too is it possible and necessary to question the claim that the United States has been and remains the standard-bearer of it. It is, after all, the contention that China seeks to break what the United States has built, and now presents itself as defending, that is identified by policymakers as the central motivation for U.S. grand strategy today. This book therefore attempts an even-handed review of what the United States and China have said, and done, in relation to the post–war order, and an open-minded inquiry into why. It begins with a consideration of international order itself—of what it is and of why states might tolerate or pursue it. A definition of the international order that is at issue today, the post–World War II international order (referred to throughout as the post–war order), follows. The definition of international order used here differs from many found elsewhere in the literature, and doubtless will be objectionable to some. It is an admittedly, but intentionally, spare rendering, a model that is meant to align with its common use in policy discourse and to provide analytical traction to what is an otherwise slippery and too-conveniently malleable idea.[23]

With this foundation in hand, the book turns to examining how the United States and China each have behaved within and in relation to the post–war order since its inception in 1945. The point of entry is a very brief look at how each nation, through the course of its intellectual history, has considered what order is and the value that it provides. There is no search for any direct effect of this lineage on the two states' foreign policies. It is, rather, simply to acknowledge that the two states arrive to their current relationship—with the post–war order, and with each other—with a different history of thought about why order is desirable and about what it requires. Making note of these differences is a useful aid to contextualizing how leaders in the United States and in China use the idea of order in their discourse today.

The book similarly makes no pretense at being a comprehensive history of U.S. or Chinese foreign policies, and neither does it presume to offer a detailed account of how any one, much less every one, of the two states' leaders have thought about, regarded, or valued the post–war order. This is not an attempt at a definitive history of leaders' thinking about the post–war order or of how their preferences and policies were shaped by the constraints and limitations placed on them by their different political systems and by the long-term convictions and short-term moods of their citizens. The effort instead is to gather sufficient information that it is possible to discern the general trend in the two states' respective relationships with the post–war order, to note deviations from it, and, on that basis, to compare their general record of conformity with or divergence from it.

The purpose is not to assail America's hypocrisy or to be apologist for its behavior, and neither is it to assail China's hypocrisy or to be apologist for its behavior. It is instead to assess the prevailing view that the United States and China have not just differing but irreconcilable positions on the future of the post–war order and to evaluate the U.S. foreign policy to which this view has led.

Such a review is merited because current U.S. foreign policy is premised on the belief that China has an appetite for dominion, on disappointment that China's internal politics have been resistant to liberalization, and on anxiety that a world in which Beijing is allowed to exercise international leadership to any greater extent than it does already will be a world hostile to liberal principles and menacing to the United States.[24] From this perspective, the costs and risks of decoupling economically, of the diplomatic work of persuading allies and partners to do the same, of investing $800 billion in military capability annually, and of loose talk about U.S. willingness to fight a war over Taiwan are not only tolerable but necessary.[25] If, however, China is not seeking to destroy the post–war order and to replace it with one that "only works for [the PRC] but not for the rest of us", then the risks U.S. foreign policy is taking might be too high.[26]

* * *

Notes

1 "A Conversation on the US Approach to the People's Republic of China with Deputy Secretary of State Wendy R. Sherman" (Washington, DC: The Brookings Institution), February 15, 2023, www.brookings.edu/events/a-conversation-on-the-us-approach-to-the-peoples-republic-of-china-with-deputy-secretary-of-state-wendy-r-sherman/.
2 Frank G. Hoffman, "Examining Complex Forms of Conflict: Grey Zone and Hybrid Challenges", *PRISM*, Vol. 7, No. 4, 2018, pp. 30–47, www.jstor.org/stable/26542705; Bonny Lin et al., "Competition in the Gray Zone: Countering China's Coercion against U.S. Allies and Partners in the Indo-Pacific" (Santa Monica, CA: RAND Corporation), 2022, https://doi.org/10.7249/RRA594-1.
3 Matias Spektor, "The Upside of Western Hypocrisy: How the Global South Can Push America to Do Better", *Foreign Affairs*, July 21, 2023, www.foreignaffairs.com/united-states/upside-western-hypocrisy-global-south-america#:~:text=Hypocrisy%20occurs%20when%20political%20leaders,United%20States%20two%20decades%20ago.
4 Robert Kagan, "War and the Liberal Hegemony", *Liberties*, Vol. 2, No. 4, Summer 2022; Christopher Preble and William Ruger, "No More of the Same: The Problem with Primacy", *War on the Rocks*, August 31, 2016, https://warontherocks.com/2016/08/no-more-of-the-same-the-problem-with-primacy/.
5 "United States National Security Strategy" (Washington, DC: The White House), October 2022, p. 8.
6 "China's Economic Rise: History, Trends, Challenges, and Implications for the United States" (Washington, DC: Congressional Research Service), June 15, 2019, www.everycrsreport.com/reports/RL33534.html#_Toc12530838; www.brookings.edu/wp-content/uploads/2016/07/China-as-a-Global-Investor_Asia-Working-Paper-4-2.pdf.
7 William Gallo, "As Trump Looms, South Koreans Mull their Own Nukes", *VOA East Asia*, November 24, 2022, www.voanews.com/a/as-trump-looms-south-koreans-mull-their-own-nukes/6848246.html; Jonathan Swan, Charlie Savage, and Maggie Haberman, "Fears of a NATO Withdrawal Rise as Trump Seeks a Return to Power", *The New York Times*, December 9, 2023, www.nytimes.com/2023/12/09/us/politics/trump-2025-nato.html.
8 Richard Fontaine, "The Myth of Neutrality: Countries Will Have to Choose between America and China", *Foreign Affairs*, July 12, 2023, www.foreignaffairs.com/china/myth-of-neutrality-choose-between-america-china; Jonathan Stromseth, "Don't Make Us Choose: Southeast Asia in the Throes of US-China Rivalry" (Washington, DC: The Brookings Institution), October 2019, www.brookings.edu/articles/dont-make-us-choose-southeast-asia-in-the-throes-of-us-china-rivalry/.
9 G. John Ikenberry, *Liberal Leviathan: The Origins, Crisis, and Transformation of the American World Order* (Princeton, NJ: Princeton University Press), 2011; Michael J. Mazarr et al., *Understanding the*

Current International Order (Santa Monica, CA: RAND Corporation), 2016, www.rand.org/pubs/research_reports/RR1598.html.

10 Robert A. Pollard, "Economic Security and the Origins of the Cold War: Bretton Woods, the Marshall Plan, and American Rearmament, 1944–50", *Diplomatic History*, Vol. 9, No. 3, 1985, pp. 271–289, www.jstor.org/stable/24911665.

11 *Convention on the Prevention and Punishment of the Crime of Genocide*, December 9, 1948, 78 U.N.T.S. 276 (entered into force January 12, 1951), https://treaties.un.org/Pages/showDetails.aspx?objid=0800000280027fac.

12 Michael J. Mazarr, "The Looming Crisis in the South China Sea", *Foreign Affairs*, February 9, 2024, www.foreignaffairs.com/united-states/looming-crisis-south-china-sea?utm_medium=newsletters&utm_source=fatoday&utm_campaign=How%20Gaza%20Reunited%20the%20Middle%20East&utm_content=20240209&utm_term=FA%20Today%20-%20112017; Ryan Hass, "What America Wants from China", *Foreign Affairs*, November/December 2023, www.foreignaffairs.com/united-states/what-america-wants-china-hass.

13 Elizabeth Economy, *The World According to China* (Medford, MA: Polity Press), 2022, pp. 2–3.

14 Elbridge Colby, *The Strategy of Denial: American Defense in an Age of Great Power Conflict* (New Haven, CT: Yale University Press), 2021, pp. 25–26.

15 Michael Schuman, "China Could Soon be the Dominant Military Power in Asia", *The Atlantic*, May 4, 2023, www.theatlantic.com/international/archive/2023/05/china-military-size-power-asia-pacific/673933/.

16 Rush Doshi, *The Long Game: China's Strategy to Displace American Order* (New York: Oxford University Press), 2021.

17 Ibid., pp. 5–6.

18 Ibid. There are many quotations provided (pp. 265–276). Some examples include: "China's strength in all aspects will continue to approach or even surpass the United States in the next 30 years"; "Although Western regimes appear to be in power, their willingness and ability to intervene in world affairs is declining. The United States may no longer want to be a provider of global security and public goods, and instead pursue a unilateral and even nationalist foreign policy"; "The international structure has become increasingly balanced"; "At present, China is in the best development period since modern times, and the world is in a state of great changes not seen in one hundred years"; "The 'great change' in 'great changes unseen in a century' is an acceleration in the redistribution of power among nations within the international structure"; "Compared with the Korean War in the 1950s, the Vietnam War in the 1960s, and international sanctions in the 1990s, China's current international difficulties are very small . . . What matters most now is how China should take advantage of this strategic opportunity", "For China, the great changes bring both challenges and opportunities . . . The

United States has regarded China as a strategic competitor, and the overall strength of the United States is still stronger than that of China. In this case, whether it can cope with the strategic competitive pressure of the United States is a severe test for China".

19 Rush Doshi, *The Long Game: China's Strategy to Displace American Order*, p. 276.
20 Ibid., pp. 59 and 263.
21 Vivian Wang and David Pierson, "In Talks with Biden, Xi Seeks to Assure and Assert at the Same Time", *The New York Times*, November 16, 2023, www.nytimes.com/2023/11/16/world/asia/china-biden-xi-summit.html.
22 Rush Doshi, *The Long Game: China's Strategy to Displace American Order*, p. 264; Michael Beckley, "Delusions of Detente: Why America and China Will Be Enduring Rivals", *Foreign Affairs*, August 22, 2023, www.foreignaffairs.com/united-states/china-delusions-detente-rivals?utm_medium=newsletters&utm_source=fatoday&utm_campaign=Delusions%20of%20D%C3%A9tente&utm_content=20230823&utm_term=FA%20Today%20-%20112017.
23 Alastair Iain Johnston's approach in his well-regarded article, "China in a World of Orders: Rethinking Compliance and Challenge in Beijing's International Relations" is, as he notes, "much messier" and likely also "more conceptually valid". The model of order used here sacrifices the latter to avoid the former. Alastair Iain Johnston, "China in a World of Orders: Rethinking Compliance and Challenge in Beijing's International Relations", *International Security*, Vol. 44, No. 2, 2019, pp. 9–60, 22, https://doi.org/10.1162/isec_a_00360.
24 Rush Doshi, *The Long Game: China's Strategy to Displace American Order*, with a crystallization of these concerns on p. 4; Elbridge Colby, *The Strategy of Denial*.
25 James Morton Turner, "The U.S. Can Counter China's Control of Minerals for the Energy Transition", *The New York Times*, November 6, 2023, www.nytimes.com/2023/11/06/opinion/electric-battery-energy-china.html.
26 "A Conversation on the US Approach to the People's Republic of China with Deputy Secretary of State Wendy R. Sherman" (Washington, DC: The Brookings Institution), February 15, 2023, www.brookings.edu/events/a-conversation-on-the-us-approach-to-the-peoples-republic-of-china-with-deputy-secretary-of-state-wendy-r-sherman/.

2

ORDER

***

The world is a chaotic place, full of people doing things everywhere and all the time. This simple fact gives rise to the two most persistent preoccupations of civilization: philosophy and government. Both are attempts to divine the most effective means of controlling the relentlessness of human activity—of shaping its day-to-day operations and of shepherding its movement over time. They are desperate attempts to impose order.

Order emerges when philosophical principles, religious or secular, are realized in widely adopted structures and practices of daily life; when they become rules that are known and enforced. Once established in practice and upheld through systems of punishment, philosophical principles become ideologies. Ideologies are potent and dangerous things. They are expressions in rhetoric and in action of conviction about the best—the "right"—way for humans to live, and to live together. They inflame passions, mobilize masses, and become fighting faiths. It is the consonance and dissonance among ideologies that define societies, and then shape how those societies will engage with each other on the full set of possibilities and problems that emerge from cohabitation on Earth.

To seek order in modern international relations is to pursue a condition in which the dominant ideologies within states do not create constant violent conflict among them, thereby allowing interstate relations to remain at least largely peaceable.[1] Individual states therefore have an interest in order generally, because it creates a predictability of affairs that allows governments to focus the majority of their attention on their own domestic politics, and because it is an enabling condition for interstate commerce. States also have an interest in order specifically, because it reduces the immediacy of the fear that their physical security and national independence are at risk.

DOI: 10.4324/9781032723358-2

Acceptance of the idea of order, however, is not the same as agreement about what an order requires, of whom, and why. In the domestic context, answering these questions is the responsibility of national governments. It is the government in whatever form—monarchy, theocracy, democracy, dictatorship, or autocracy—that sets the rules about how its citizens are, and are not, to dispatch their duties to the state and to engage with one another in society. In the international context, establishing rules is the responsibility of no one. This is not to say that international relations are therefore always and in all ways disordered and chaotic. To the contrary, there have been periods, some of them prolonged, during which relations among states have been quite structured and routinized.[2]

These periods have featured a consistency across state behaviors, some of which can be associated with, or even attributed to, agreements made between and among them in the form of treaties: official statements that tie specific actions to particular responses, to be undertaken by a designated entity endowed with the authority to do so. Treaties and their terms are therefore often understood to establish the rules of international affairs. Because no one state has a monopoly on the possession or use of violence to impose its will, however, states are not really bound by these rules unless they choose to be. Treaties are entered into by choice and are built through the often long and laborious processes of multilateral negotiation and domestic legislation, both of which are meant to ensure substantive alignment, to demonstrate seriousness of intent, and to increase the consequence of breaking them. Some treaties in international relations are called international law, though there is no strict or generally accepted definition of when and which treaties become international law, and even these are accepted, rejected, and enforced by states at their discretion.

Norms are often referred to in tandem with rules, though they are comparatively less firmly defined, more informal, and liable to such existential questions as "How do we know a norm when we see one? How do we know norms make a difference in politics? Where do norms come from? How do they change?"[3] Treaties might therefore be said to give an international order its structure, and norms its character. There can be consequences for defying a rule or a norm, insofar as one or more of those interested in perpetuating it is willing and able to levy those consequences. When no enforcer emerges and punishment is not forthcoming, however, or when the recipient of punishment is unmoved, then the rule or norm will bifurcate, with some adhering to it and others not, or it can break altogether.[4]

In the West, after centuries of religious wars, wars of empire, and the treaties that ended one before the next began, the geographic reach and technology-fueled carnage of World War I brought a special urgency to the desire to get hold of order on the European continent once and for all. The war's end was codified in the 1919 Treaty of Versailles, the terms of which were subject to criticism then and since, but the effort to extend cessation of that one war into prevention of all other wars continued for the decade that followed. Whether hopelessly utopian in its vision or hopelessly realpolitik in its design, the goal of the internationalist League of Nations, established in 1920, was to create order by enmeshing the countries of the world in an institution that would preserve peace through the exercise of legal procedure and military enforcement of judgments rendered.[5] The Paris Peace Pact—or Kellogg-Briand Pact as it is known in the United States—that followed eight years later was equally global in its expression, defining war wherever it occurred as an illegal act. Neither the League nor the Pact prevented the outbreak of World War II in 1939.

The League of Nations was not the only attempt to make war obsolete that was defined by earnest intent, ironic effect, and abject failure. Alfred Nobel, the inventor of dynamite who lived and died before World War I, having appreciated its use for destructive purpose in wartime longed "to produce a substance or a machine of such frightful efficacy for wholesale devastation that it would make wars altogether impossible", one that would bring all civilized nations to "recoil from war in horror and disband their forces".[6] This belief, that it was only recognition of the profound inhumanity of war that could produce its abolition, was so sincere that Nobel himself worked to design and test new such weapons of frightful efficacy—producing torpedoes, rockets, and biological agents—before turning his sizable fortune to rewarding endeavors that sought peace through other, non-munitions-based applications of science.

Scientists of course did go on to create weapons of frightful efficacy in the form of nuclear weapons. As had been true for Nobel's work, these weapons succeeded in making war ever more capable of causing wholesale devastation yet they, too, also failed to make it "altogether impossible". Nonetheless, their use by the United States over two cities in Japan to end World War II did bring not only another special urgency but also a new sobriety to the work of creating a post–war order.

The Post–World War II Order

Influential narratives in the United States today present the post–World War II order as having been politically liberalizing in intent and purposefully beneficent from the beginning, built "because we recognized that it would serve humanity's interest, but also our own".[7] They find the origins of its liberal ethos in Woodrow Wilson's call to make the world safe for democracy and in President Franklin D. Roosevelt's January 1941 State of the Union address, in which he famously expressed his hope for "a world founded upon four essential human freedoms": those of expression and worship, and from want and fear. The Atlantic Charter that Roosevelt signed in August 1941 with U.K. Prime Minister Winston Churchill, however, in which the two leaders articulated principles they would wish to guide international relations after the war's eventual end, was mostly pragmatic.[8] Its provisions included an intolerance for territorial aggression and support for national self-determination, freedom of the seas, and non-discriminatory trade agreements. The Charter also hinted at the pursuit of global economic development and of global disarmament, though it included no means through which to achieve the latter other than states simply doing so of their own accord.[9]

Roosevelt himself may have been sincere in his desire to see Western conceptions of human well-being and liberty define the global order, but that was not ultimately the order to which he and his successors affixed the United States after the war's end.[10] That order, the product of years of negotiation among the wartime allies and of intense political wrangling inside of them, was of dual construction, with contours that resembled republicanism embedded in a structure that operated through the practices of power politics. Its purpose, moreover, was not to better the human condition worldwide by bringing the internal politics of states to more closely resemble liberal democracy or to be newly protective of human rights, but to do so first, and simply, by making great power war—the kind of war that became world war—less likely.[11] To achieve this, the post–war order was designed to address what were understood to have been the antecedents of those wars: pursuit of national economic interests through parochialism and protectionism and the absence of impediments to the use of force.

What emerged therefore was an order structured around two ideas and four institutions. The first idea was free-trade, the second was multilateralism, and the four institutions—the World Bank, the International Monetary Fund (IMF), the General Agreement on Tariffs and Trade (GATT) (now the World Trade Organization), and the United Nations (U.N.)—were founded to put those ideas into practice.

Free-trade multilateralism is eponymous—it largely is what it says that it is. Its core economic premise is that the relatively unencumbered exchange of money, goods, and services generates national productivity and wealth. Its core political premise is that multilateral management of these and other state interactions, codified in treaties and administered through institutions, makes war less likely. Free-trade multilateralism thus deeply embeds liberal economic theories into its operation but not political ones. To the contrary, the United Nations was built precisely because differences among states' internal ideologies, and especially and most dangerously among the ideologies of the great powers, was an accepted reality. The institution's purpose was not to mold them into conformity but rather to achieve "the elimination of war by the substitution of other techniques for the settlement of international controversies".[12] While some of the post–war order's architects might also have believed that economic liberalism would breed political liberalism, this was not the dominant view at the time and neither was it the project's express intent.

It was quickly understood, however, that the free-trade regime would apply to only half of the world—the rest, dominated by the Soviet Union and its communist ideology, would be closed to the economies of the West. This didn't mean that there would be no global post–war order, but it did mean that the truly global operation of free-trade multilateralism would have to wait.

Free-Trade Multilateralism

The three treaty-based economic institutions founded in the aftermath of World War II were designed to be forums for negotiation of finance needs and trade deals, founded on principles of reciprocity and transparency, attached to mechanisms for raising and remedying issues, interests, and objections. The purpose was not to generate global economic wealth. It was to create an international economic system that might prevent recurrence of the kinds of chronic grievances and acute disagreements that had so recently contributed to crushing economic crisis and culminated in catastrophic war. Achieving this objective would require balancing the need of national governments to manage their own economies in order to maintain sociopolitical stability—to avoid civic unrest and minimize opportunity for the emergence of another round of virulent nationalism—but without creating effects that were so damaging to other nations that they initiated a chain reaction of mutually destructive practices.[13] The post-war financial order thus coupled rules and regulations with special arrangements (including those derived from colonialism), exceptions, and allowances for "emergency actions" where necessary in the "quest for domestic stability".[14]

The theory that the post-war economic institutions put into practice is that trade, mostly unburdened by taxes levied on imports in the form of tariffs, and mostly undistorted by preferential investments of government funds in the form of subsidies, fosters healthy competition and an equilibrium based on comparative advantage. Conditions of openness, in other words, allow the market forces of supply, demand, and the costs of production to determine what an economy produces and what it purchases. Free trade thus is most efficient when it draws upon a diverse set of economies, a large market characterized by variation in allotments of physical and human capital and natural resources.

The coupling of free trade with multilateral institutions was meant to tether the jumble of interacting market forces between and among its diverse participants to a stable base. This was to be done by providing a common understanding of what distinguishes legitimate domestic economic policy from protectionism, and about which trade restrictions are justified and acceptable and which are discriminatory and destructive. Stability in free trade multilateralism is also contingent upon participants having shared expectations about the financial terms of exchange: about the relative values of national currencies, about the limits of acceptable risk in the cross-border movement of those currencies, and about whether and how domestic financial crises with international implications are to be addressed.

U.S. insistence on these features reflected the belief that low barriers to trade and open financial flows were to the benefit of the resource-rich United States—conducive to its economic goals of productivity and growth—but also that free and open multilateralism was to the benefit of all participants, economically and as a means of reducing the sources of conflict.[15] Whatever the distribution of conviction and interest among U.S. negotiators on these points, a sufficient case was made and sufficient leverage applied that an emphasis on low barriers to trade, open financial flows, and institutional oversight were foundational features of the structure that emerged from negotiations about the post-war economic order, in the form of the Bretton Woods Agreement.

The World Bank

Signed in 1944 by 43 nations, Bretton Woods created a division of labor among institutions charged with managing the international economy. The World Bank was to grow the pool of nations capable of participating in international commerce first by overseeing multinational investment in the redevelopment of the war-battered countries of Europe and then, when the Marshall Plan assumed responsibility for European reconstruction, to fund development in other states around the world.[16] The World Bank dispatched this duty primarily by providing loans at rates unavailable from private lenders, initially drawn from funds contributed by its member states and administered by the International Bank for Reconstruction and Development (IBRD).[17] The IBRD was joined in 1955 by the International Finance Corporation (IFC) and in 1960 by the International Development Association (IDA), now collectively known as the World Bank Group, with the former attending to direct investments in companies and the latter distributing grants with less demanding interest rates and repayment terms.[18]

These modes of redistributing global finance were deployed together with technical advice and counsel. In the World Bank's early years, it was focused on projects officials considered useful to building physical infrastructure that wasn't attractive to private investors because of its scale and lengthy time horizons. In later years the Bank would emphasize projects that had the potential to contribute to economic growth and to do so while encouraging the adoption of liberal economic practices.[19] This evolution reflected a philosophy in which infrastructure and economic liberalism were understood to be the necessary precursors of the domestic accumulation of capital that was needed for a state to become both an active importer and exporter. Wealth at home would produce an increase in individual consumption, which would generate local production and create a market for imports. The creation of a robust consumer base would in turn attract investment in local industries that would over time become a country's export base. All of which is to say, these redistributions of multilateral funds were pursued because it was believed that they would assist developing countries in demonstrating their potential for private consumption and collective productivity. This would make them more attractive to private investment, which would then provide capital on more tenable terms, which would then make recipient nations more able to participate in interstate trade, which would then grow their economies, and so the virtuous cycle would go.[20]

The International Monetary Fund

The International Monetary Fund (IMF), also founded at Bretton Woods, was the institution charged with establishing a shared set of expectations about the monetary practices that would make the cross-border flow of money, goods, and services sufficiently stable, but without also being so rigid as to disincentivize companies from investing or governments from borrowing from sources abroad.[21] At its inception, the IMF oversaw a monetary system that operated by fixing exchange rates. The Fund marked the value of a national currency managed by a central bank—the financial institution within each country responsible for printing and distributing the nation's money—against the U.S. dollar. The U.S. dollar was itself marked against the value of gold.

Central banks were expected to buy and sell their own currencies in order to maintain a price within 1% on either side of their dollar-pegged values and were not to adjust that pegged-price absent IMF approval.[22] When a state was at risk of needing to considerably devalue its currency in order to meet the peg—meaning that it would require more of that nation's own currency to purchase one U.S. dollar—the IMF would provide loans. This was necessary to avoid steep increases in inflation, which would make that country's citizens poorer and therefore unhappier. In extreme cases, countries could be at risk of having their currency become essentially valueless, which would cause economic collapse and all of the terrible and frightening social consequences thereof. In this way, the IMF was meant to provide a stabilizing set of rules to govern international monetary behavior and to serve as a stopgap when central banks were in real trouble.

Bretton Woods established the dollar as the reserve currency, the asset held by all other states in the monetary system and therefore the easiest medium of exchange. This was at least to some degree a default outcome, as the U.S. economy was by far the post-war period's largest, and no other truly suitable alternative was available.[23] This changed over time, however, as the European and Japanese economies recovered, and the United States experienced a period of high inflation in the late 1960s and early 1970s.

For two decades, the Bretton Woods balancing act had been maintained by allowing states enough control over their own currencies to be responsive to inflation and unemployment, but not so much as to privilege them to the extent that they would undermine the economies of others—the currency pegs hindered a country from artificially making exports of its own goods so cheap that it effectively destroyed those same industries elsewhere. Bretton Woods achieved this in part by attaching the U.S. dollar to gold. This was the so-called gold standard, and it created a reference category against which all other currencies could then be valued.

But by 1971, the U.S. dollar had become too easy to spend abroad and too expensive for others to buy. The result was an increase in U.S. imports, a decrease in its exports, and inflation in the domestic economy.[24] Banks holding large amounts of U.S. dollars therefore had reason to anticipate that the United States, under the leadership of the Nixon administration, might move to devalue the dollar—to make each one worth less gold tomorrow than it was worth today. This gave them reason to cash in today, not tomorrow, and some of them began to do so. If too many banks called in their chits, however, the administration would have no control over the pace or extent of devaluation. The dollar could fall fast and far, and the U.S. economy might crash. Nixon could try to preempt these dynamics by raising interest rates, making U.S. businesses and consumers less eager to spend, but this introduced the risk of recession. Even if it didn't, Nixon had ample political incentive not to ask Americans to endure a period of economic slowdown immediately prior to the 1972 presidential election.

The other option was simply to sever the tie between the U.S. dollar and an ounce of gold. This would give the United States more control over its monetary policy and solve the problem of gold buyouts. In August 1971, this is what the Nixon administration did, delinking the U.S. dollar from gold and thereby bringing the Bretton Woods regime to an end. This decision had two implications. The first was practical: it pulled the pin out of the Bretton Woods system, untethering world finance from any agreed standard of value and allowing the market forces of supply and demand to determine what any one currency was worth in terms of any other. The second implication was one of principle: dropping the gold standard meant that the United States was breaking faith with the effort to hold in sustainable tension domestic socio-economic health and the second- and third-order effects of maintaining that health on the socio-economic health of other nations.

After a turbulent two years of adjustment, the financial system recalibrated. Central banks have since been at liberty to float their exchange rate so that it is wholly responsive to market forces, or to fix it against another state's or set of states' currencies, or even to adopt the currency of another country as their own. Over the next four decades, this system produced the kinds of dangerous turmoil the early overseers of Bretton Woods had sought to avoid. Governments began to print more currency, which fueled inflation, and currency speculators bought and sold in ways that created crises and near-collapses in Europe and Latin America in the late 1980s and throughout East Asia, Russia, and Brazil in the 1990s. But the IMF and national governments responded to defend against further contagion that would threaten the overall operation of the international economy, restructuring debt and infusing money into the most severely affected states. It did so again after the global financial crisis of 2008.[25] Thus although the U.S. break from the gold-standard was an act of economic nationalism, it was not accompanied by a withdrawal from the IMF or a general dissolution of that institution, leaving the principle of economic multilateralism intact.

The World Bank and the IMF continue to operate in tandem to develop and enforce rules about which governments can receive their loans, under what conditions, and with which requirements attached. These rules are set and decisions made by various configurations of leadership boards, and the institutions' members have weighted voting rights set on the basis of their financial contributions. Both enforce their rules by structuring their loans with periodic reviews, audits, and investigations. The IMF can withhold funds when states are in breach of loan requirements, and the World Bank maintains a sanctions regime that it can impose when states are found to be guilty of fraudulent or corrupt use of its funds.

The General Agreement on Tariffs and Trade

The post-war planners intended for the World Bank's development mandate and the IMF's stabilization mandate to be joined by an organization with a rules-of-free-trade mandate. It was initially conceived as the International Trade Organization (ITO), for which the United States presented a draft Charter to 17 other countries in 1946.[26] Negotiations proceeded through 1948.

The U.S. delegation worked throughout to balance the often contradictory imperatives of the American commitment to multilateral free trade with the realities of economic reconstruction in Europe and the need of developing nations—as expressed most vigorously by Australia, India, and China—to grow nascent productive sectors. Both groups desired and were allowed protections from their more competitive counterparts in the industrialized world. Although U.S. officials initially were guarded about appearing to exclude the Soviet Union from participation in the trade regime, this reservation gave way as contestation grew between U.S.-style liberal capitalist economics and Soviet-style centrally planned communism. As negotiations proceeded, the United States became increasingly committed to ensuring that the ITO was more associated with the former than it was with the latter.[27] For their labors, the U.S. delegation succeeded in negotiating an ITO charter in 1948 that, despite their satisfaction with its "strong sense of American authorship", in 1949 failed even to be sent to the U.S. Congress because it was clear that ratification would not be forthcoming—with the exception of one of its chapters.[28] That chapter was titled the General Agreement on Tariffs and Trade (GATT).

From its modest beginnings as a positive externality of an intended but ultimately unrealized instrument, the GATT rather overachieved. Its initial members made huge reductions in tariffs, signing "over a hundred agreements, affecting more than forty-five thousand tariffs that covered about half of world trade".[29] It entrenched the principle of non-discrimination, committing participants to extend their best terms of trade, as negotiated with any one member state, to all member states.

The GATT lasted for 45 years before evolving into the World Trade Organization (WTO) in 1994. During its tenure, the GATT established itself as an operative, representative multilateral organization, endured through four protracted and contentious rounds of negotiation that produced further reductions of barriers to trade and expanded from 23 to 164 members.[30] Whether the GATT and then the WTO achieved the objective of expanding global free trade or simply were coincident with it, it is indisputable that these organizations were manifestations of their member states' commitment to a multilateral approach to at least trying to do so, and to doing so in ways that might prevent economic disagreement from becoming armed conflict.[31]

The rules that emerge from the WTO, what it calls "agreements", are the products of negotiations among some, many, or all of its member states and enter into force so long as no member actively objects. A state that believes a signatory to an agreement is in violation of its rules can lodge a claim with the WTO's Dispute Settlement Body for resolution. If that body finds the rules have been broken, and the rule-breaker does not correct its violation, then the state that filed the claim can apply its own retaliatory measures in an effort to enforce compliance—and, if correction of the bad behavior is not forthcoming, then at least to staunch its losses. It is not the expectation that these mechanisms will always produce good-spirited or even grudgingly accepted compromise, but the hope is that they at a minimum will provide sufficient procedural justice to quell states' impulses toward more dangerous reactions.

However optimistic, or even just hopeful, the post-war planners were that the World Bank, IMF and GATT/WTO would reduce the likelihood of interstate conflict, they also understood that these institutions were unlikely to suffice to address any or all reasons a state might resort to force. States fight to control and maintain sources of prosperity, but prosperous states also fight about other things.

The United Nations

The United Nations was formed in 1945 to be the ultimate arbiter for if and when the economic institutions proved unable to reconcile their disagreements, and as a means of trying to make real in state policy the agreement in principle that war is not an accepted means of settling disputes, whether about religion, royalty, identity, ideology, treasure, territory, or honor. The U.N.'s mandate thus is to be an alternative to violence by rendering and enforcing judgment about the proper resolution of conflicts of interest that states are either unwilling or unable to resolve themselves. Stated more specifically by one scholar, "the primary purpose of the United Nations [is] to 'maintain international peace and security'", and this is visible in three types of activities the United Nations has undertaken since its founding: "normative development concerning the non-use of force, nonintervention, and peaceful change; the creation of specific international rules governing levels and types of national armaments; and the management of actual conflicts among states".[32]

The U.N.'s global scope was a reaction to the belief that exclusive alliances and balance-of-power politics were implicated in both world wars, but its design was an acknowledgment that power relationships would continue to matter, very much. The United Nations thus is an intentionally hybrid construction, an amalgam of modern democratic pluralism and retrograde great power politics. Its General Assembly (GA) is composed of the full roster of member states, each with equal status and standing, and one vote. The Assembly "is the organization's primary deliberative body" and "may discuss or make recommendations on any questions or issues within the scope of the U.N. Charter, including the powers and functions" of other of the U.N.'s constituent bodies.[33] GA resolutions, however, are "recommendatory in nature and nonbinding".[34]

The General Assembly also elects rotational members onto the U.N. Security Council (UNSC), adding representatives from 10 states on a staggered two-year cycle to the Council's permanent major power concert of five members (P5): the United States, China, France, Russia, and the United Kingdom.[35] The UNSC has the power to call states into conflict negotiations, deploy peacekeeping forces in conflict zones, impose economic or diplomatic sanctions, and authorize the use of force.[36] The five permanent members of the Security Council also have veto power, which they can exercise, for any reason at all, over any substantive resolution forwarded for decision within the Council. Although the veto has been subject to regular criticism—for the inequality it builds into the United Nations and, often, for the manner of its exercise—it serves the essential purpose of acknowledging that in the absence of some mechanism for pursuing divergent interests inside the institution the major powers are likely to leave and pursue those interests outside of it.[37]

Just as the U.N. Charter built into its structure a contradiction between the principle of the General Assembly's juridical equality and the reality of the Security Council's status inequality, so too does it contain a contradiction between the principles of sovereign right and sovereign obligation. In its most spare rendering, sovereignty refers to

the exercise of control by an identified authority over a defined territory, with or without people in it. This definition implies that respect for
sovereignty includes allowing a government full latitude in setting and
enforcing the rules that apply within the territory over which it exercises
control. Yet the U.N. Charter also appends that right with the obligation that although states need not always work in the interests of their
peoples, they at least cannot commit systematic acts of violence against
them. The sovereign right of states is codified in Article 2.7, worded as
a mutual agreement not to intervene in another state's internal affairs,
while the obligation of states not to ignore or negate the humanity of its
citizens is found in its textual affirmations of "the dignity and worth of
the human person, in equal rights of men and women", and in the now
numerous declarations, conventions, and treaties that have been added
since and are generally referred to as protections of human rights.[38]

The conceptual difficulties that emerge in any attempt to reconcile
the two have preoccupied legal scholars ever since and increasingly are
a source of contestation among states. Their respective definitions are
unfixed, the rights and duties that they convey are matters of interpretation, and it is unclear which takes precedence over the other. These
characteristics mean that states often justify their behaviors on the basis
of the one, or of the other, seeking not only to further their immediate
interests but also to set a precedent that they believe will serve their
purposes into the future.

Defend or Degrade

The great powers have stayed in the U.N. and the other post-war institutions despite their internal dilemmas. Beyond just persisting, they
have spawned imitators—over time, they have been complemented and
supplemented by other institutions. Multilateral defense organizations,
most prominently the highly institutionalized North Atlantic Treaty
Organization (NATO) (and, when it existed, its Cold War foil the War-
saw Pact), is an insurance policy that reflects its members' insecurity
that their independent state arsenals and the U.N., even together, are
sufficient disincentive for a war of aggression. Other institutions, like the
Organization for Economic Co-operation and Development (OECD),
the African Union (AU), the Organization of Petroleum Exporting
Countries (OPEC), the World Health Organization (WHO), the International Atomic Energy Agency (IAEA), and the Asian Infrastructure
and Investment Bank (AIIB), among many others, address interests and
issues that are region, resource, or function specific. These institutions
are formed when states believe their needs require attention of a type or

to an extent that exceed the purview or the capabilities of the original post-war institutions, or when they conclude that those institutions are simply unwilling to address them.[39]

Each of these and all the other estimated 500 intergovernmental institutions that exist today do so to try to set rules, and they have their own rules about how rules are set, about how they are enforced, and about who enforces them.[40] The dissolution of any one of them would have functional implications and of more than one simultaneously or in rapid succession would be a troubling indicator of a diminished willingness among states to seek cooperative solutions to shared problems. The obsolescence—either as a result of paralysis within, state withdrawal from, or the complete collapse of—one or more of the post-war institutions, however, would be of a different order and magnitude. Such an outcome would reveal the loss of collective belief that the practices of free-trade and the tools of multilateralism can prevent great power war.

If the post-war institutions are working effectively, then the overlap between their rules and the principles they were founded to promote will be large. If it is not, then the converse will be true. If institutional rules have large overlap with principles, then defending the post–war order requires rhetorically reinforcing its principles, expressing support for its institutions, generally following their rules, and acting to enforce them even when others do not. If institutional rules have low overlap, however, then defending the order demands more. It demands that states speak on behalf of and behave consistently with the post-war principles of their own volition and that they work to fix the rules to achieve better alignment.

Challenging the post–war order—seeking to break it or to replace it—logically means the opposite. A state that seeks to degrade the post–war order would be expected to express little or no fealty to the post–war order in its rhetoric, and in action to use the post-war institutions only instrumentally or opportunistically. Such a state would be far more likely simply to ignore the institutions' rules than to invest in the work of rewriting them and might even agitate for the creation of an entirely new construct for ordering international affairs. Russia under Vladimir Putin, for example, has both long objected to the continuation of the post–war order and has repeatedly disregarded its prohibition on territorial aggression and on interfering in the domestic political affairs of others.[41]

Figure 2.1 visualizes the qualitative approach used to assess whether a state's behavior is more indicative of an intent to defend the international order or to degrade it. The image diagrams the overlap among the principles of the post–war order, the rules of the post-war institutions, and state behavior.

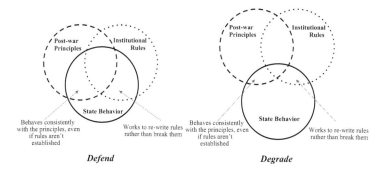

FIGURE 2.1   Evaluating Compliance with the Post–War Order

Source: Created by the author.

It is neither necessary nor possible to assess the quality or quantity of state fealty to the post–war order's principles or adherence to its institutions' rules against a standard of perfection. Rules can be poorly specified or ambiguous, interpretations can differ, and allegations of rule violations therefore can legitimately be contested. It is far more practical instead to apply the standard advised by scholars of international regimes when assessing treaty effectiveness, which they analogize to the enforcement of speed limits:

> Most communities and law enforcement organizations in the United States seem to be perfectly comfortable with a situation in which the average speed on interstate highways is perhaps ten miles above the limit. . . . The fundamental problem of the system is not how to induce drivers to obey the speed limit but how to contain deviance within acceptable levels. So, too, it is for international treaty obligations.[42]

Applying the "deviance within acceptable levels" approach to evaluating state defiance and compliance with the post–war order means making judgments not at a level of detail, but rather at some level of aggregation; the concern is with the large muscle movements, not the exercise of fine motor control. Russia's flagrant uses of force to subvert Georgian (2008) and Ukrainian sovereignty (2015, 2022), for example, are clear and obvious indicators of Russian disregard for the post–war order. China's short of war military coercion in its surrounding seas, by comparison, is dangerous and dislikable but still fundamentally a test of limits, not a clear violation of them.

In the absence of meaningful quantitative measures, it is to be expected that different analysts will render different qualitative judgments about what constitutes "deviance within acceptable levels". This work does not pretend otherwise; it simply attempts to provide a framework within which to review compliance and defiance with the post–war order and to make transparent the reasoning that leads to its conclusions about the United States and China.

* * *

Notes

1 There is a rich literature that interrogates the essence of order—whether it is an accumulation of rational choices made by individual states that together form an equilibrium, whether it is evidence of a natural sense of "society" that resides in individuals and is expressed in state policies, or whether it is produced by the exercise of force either absolutely or for purposes of upholding constructed international norms and laws. Some of these works will be addressed in this chapter; others not referenced here directly can be found in Sources Consulted.

2 Hedley Bull, *The Anarchical Society: A Study of Order in World Politics* (New York: Columbia University Press), 1977; David Kang, *East Asia before the West: Five Centuries of Trade and Tribute* (New York: Columbia University Press), 2010; Henry Kissinger, *World Order* (New York: Penguin Books), 2015.

3 Martha Finnemore and Kathryn Sikkink, "International Norm Dynamics and Political Change", *International Organization*, Vol. 52, No. 4, 1998, pp. 887–917, www.jstor.org/stable/2601361.

4 Diana Panke and Ulrich Petersohn, "Norm Challenges and Norm Death", *Cooperation and Conflict*, Vol. 51, No. 1, March 2016, pp. 3–19.

5 Oona A. Hathaway and Scott J. Shapiro, *The Internationalists: How a Radical Plan to Outlaw War Remade the World* (New York: Simon & Schuster Paperbacks), 2017; Robert Kagan, *The Ghost at the Feast: America and the Collapse of World Order, 1900–1941* (New York: Alfred A. Knopf), 2023, pp. 227–234.

6 Hertha Pauli, "Nobel's Prizes and the Atom Bomb", *Commentary*, December 1945, www.commentary.org/articles/hertha-pauli/nobels-prizes-and-the-atom-bomb/; Margaret MacMillan, *War: How Conflict Shaped Us* (New York: Random House), 2021. Nobel's conviction that weapons of "frightful efficacy" would convince all governments to avoid war extends (whether knowingly or not) ethicist and philosopher Immanuel Kant's logic that an increase in the number of democracies in the world will produce a decrease in the incidence of war—because wars are less likely to happen when the decision for it or against it is made by those who will directly suffer its costs.

7 "The Power and Purpose of American Diplomacy in a New Era", Secretary Antony J. Blinken Remarks to the Johns Hopkins School of Advanced International Studies (SAIS) (Washington, DC: The U.S. Department of State), September 13, 2023, www.state. gov/secretary-antony-j-blinken-remarks-to-the-johns-hopkins-school-of-advanced-international-studies-sais-the-power-and-purpose-of-american-diplomacy-in-a-new-era/.

8 "Franklin D. Roosevelt, Address to Congress", January 6, 1941.

9 "The Atlantic Charter: Declaration of Principles Issued by the President of the United States and the Prime Minister of the United Kingdom", August 14, 1941.

10 G. John Ikenberry, *A World Safe for Democracy: Liberal Internationalism and the Crises of Global Order* (New Haven, CT: Yale University Press), 2020, p. xi.

11 Although the proceedings of the International Military Tribunal (IMT) at Nuremberg after the war are now very much associated with the concepts of "war crimes" and "crimes against humanity", and as the trial of those directly culpable for the systematic murder of millions of Jewish people in the Holocaust, neither was the core of the prosecution. The IMT, at the insistence of the Americans involved, was instead focused primarily on "crimes against peace"—the act of armed invasion. As described in one history of the events,

The American prosecutors were determined—in disregard of international precedent and of conventional legal norms—to present the United States itself as a 'victim' of the defendants' chief 'crimes'. As the American prosecutors argued the cases, the top Nazis deserved to be punished for plotting a campaign of aggressive war—a plot so far-reaching that it ultimately dragged a reluctant America into the European conflict.

The influence of the Nuremberg trials on the United Nations, moreover, came after the creation of the institution's Charter in 1945, with the concepts of "war crimes" and "crimes against humanity" becoming embedded in the form of the Universal Declaration of Human Rights in 1948. See: Jeremy Rabkin, "Nuremberg Misremembered", *SAIS Review (1989–2003)*, Vol. 19, No. 2, 1999, pp. 81–96, 86, www.jstor.org/stable/45345840; Oona A. Hathaway and Scott J. Shapiro, *The Internationalists: How a Radical Plan to Outlaw War Remade the World*, pp. 252–305.

12 James Thomas Shotwell, as quoted in Oona A. Hathaway and Scott J. Shapiro, *The Internationalists*, p. 196.

13 Francine McKenzie, "Peace, Prosperity and Planning Postwar Trade, 1942–1948", in Michel Christian, Sandrine Kott, and Ondřej Matějka, Eds., *Planning in Cold War Europe: Competition, Cooperation, Circulations (1950s–1970s)* (Berlin/Boston, MA: De Gruyter), 2018, 1st ed., pp. 21–44, www.jstor.org/stable/j.ctvbkjvbs.4.

14 John Gerard Ruggie, "International Regimes, Transactions, and Change: Embedded Liberalism in the Postwar Economic Order",

International Organization, Vol. 36, No. 2, 1982, pp. 379–415, www.jstor.org/stable/2706527.

15 David Fromkin, *In the Time of the Americans* (New York: Vintage Books), 1995, pp. 690–691; Jeffry A. Frieden, *Global Capitalism: Its Fall and Rise in the Twentieth Century, and its Stumbles in the Twenty-First* (New York: W.W. Norton & Company), 2020, pp. 254–260.

16 Initially the European Recovery Program, the Marshall Plan was administered from 1948 to 1951 by the Economic Cooperation Administration, a U.S. entity, and its European counterpart, the Organization for European Economic cooperation. For a thorough account of the operations and importance of the Marshall Plan, see: "The Marshall Plan: Design, Accomplishments, and Significance" (Washington, DC: Congressional Research Service), January 18, 2018, www.everycrsreport.com/files/20180118_R45079_1ac1da1f6 7d80fba262ea260914c9148ba55f87a.pdf.

17 For a time, the bank also served as a guarantor of private loans, though this practice subsided very quickly in favor of the bank exercising independent judgment about the projects in which it would invest. See: Michael Gavin and Dani Rodrik, "The World Bank in Historical Perspective", *The American Economic Review*, Vol. 85, No. 2, 1995, pp. 329–334, www.jstor.org/stable/2117942.

18 These entities together with the Multilateral Investment Guarantee Agency (MIGA), and the International Centre for Settlement of Investment Disputes (ICSID) now are collectively referred to as the World Bank Group.

19 Jeffry A. Frieden, *Global Capitalism: Its Fall and Rise in the Twentieth Century, and its Stumbles in the Twenty-First*, pp. 258–259.

20 Views at the World Bank about the kinds of investments that would be most effective in signaling to the private markets varied over time, shifting away from infrastructure and toward human capital in the 1970s, for example. See Michael Gavin and Dani Rodrik, "The World Bank in Historical Perspective".

21 Jeffry A. Frieden, *Global Capitalism: Its Fall and Rise in the Twentieth Century, and its Stumbles in the Twenty-First*, p. 291.

22 Jeffry A. Frieden, *Global Capitalism: Its Fall and Rise in the Twentieth Century, and its Stumbles in the Twenty-First*, p. 257; "The International Monetary Fund" (Washington, DC: Congressional Research Service), May 24, 2018, www.everycrsreport.com/ files/20180524_R42019_23ba514c7923dda8aceb921e063a038085 f7cbc6.pdf.

23 Jeffry A. Frieden, *Global Capitalism: Its Fall and Rise in the Twentieth Century, and its Stumbles in the Twenty-First*, pp. 254–262.

24 "The International Monetary Fund".

25 Ibid.

26 Richard Toye, "Developing Multilateralism: The Havana Charter and the Fight for the International Trade Organization, 1947–48", *The International History Review*, Vol. 25, No. 2, June 2003, p. 282;

Francine McKenzie, "Peace, Prosperity and Planning Postwar Trade, 1942–1948".

27 Jeffry A. Frieden, *Global Capitalism: Its Fall and Rise in the Twentieth Century, and its Stumbles in the Twenty-First*, p. 263.

28 Francine McKenzie, "Peace, Prosperity and Planning Postwar Trade, 1942–1948", p. 34.

29 Jeffry A. Frieden, *Global Capitalism: Its Fall and Rise in the Twentieth Century, and its Stumbles in the Twenty-First*, p. 288.

30 The GATT did include an opt-out clause as follows:
      This Agreement . . . shall not apply as between any contracting party and any other contracting party if: a) the two contracting parties have not entered into tariff negotiations with each other, and b) either of the contracting parties, at the time either becomes a contracting party, does not consent to such application.
      General Agreement on Tariffs and Trade, Article XXXV, Non-Application of the Agreement between particular Contracting Parties.

31 Andrew K. Rose, "Do We Really Know That the WTO Increases Trade?", *The American Economic Review*, Vol. 94, No. 1, March 2004, pp. 98–114; Judith L. Goldstein, Douglas Rivers, and Michael Tomz, "Institutions in International Relations: Understanding the Effects of the GATT and the WTO on World Trade", *International Organization*, Vol. 61, No. 1, 2007, pp. 37–67, www.jstor.org/stable/4498137.

32 John Gerard Ruggie, "The United States and the United Nations: Toward a New Realism", *International Organization*, Vol. 39, No. 2, 1985, pp. 343–356, www.jstor.org/stable/2706713.

33 "The United Nations System: Frequently Asked Questions" (Washington, DC: Congressional Research Service), September 22, 2023, p. 2, https://sgp.fas.org/crs/row/R47715.pdf.

34 Ibid.

35 David L. Bosco, "Assessing the U.N. Security Council: A Concert Perspective", *Global Governance*, Vol. 20, No. 4, 2014, pp. 545–561.

36 "The United Nations System".

37 Jan Wouters and Tom Ruys, "Use and Abuse of the Veto Power", *Security Council Reform: A New Veto for a New Century?* (Brussels: Egmont Institute), 2005, www.jstor.org/stable/resrep06699.5; John Trent and Laura Schnurr, "Evolving International Organizations: The U.N. Past and Present", in John Trent and Laura Schnurr, Eds., *A United Nations Renaissance: What the U.N. Is, and What it Could Be* (Leverkusen: Verlag Barbara Budrich), 2018, 1st ed., pp. 22–55, https://doi.org/10.2307/j.ctvdf03xp.6.

38 John Trent and Laura Schnurr, "Evolving International Organizations: The U.N. Past and Present".

39 The WHO and IAEA are part of the UN System—two of its 15 Specialized Agencies—but all of the specialized agencies operate independently of the U.N. itself.

40 Mette Eilstrup-Sangiovanni, "Death of International Organizations: The Organizational Ecology of Intergovernmental Organizations,

1815–2015", *The Review of International Organizations*, Vol. 15, 2020, pp. 339–370, https://doi.org/10.1007/s11558-018-9340-5.

41 Elias Gotz and Camille-Renaud Merlen, "Russia and the Question of World Order", *European Politics and Society*, Vol. 20, No. 2, 2019, pp. 133–153, https://doi.org/10.1080/23745118.2018.1545181.

42 Abram Chayes and Antonia Handler Chayes, "On Compliance", *International Organization*, Vol. 47, No. 2, 1993, pp. 175–205, 197–198, www.jstor.org/stable/2706888. They contend, moreover, that "what is 'acceptable' in terms of compliance will reflect the perspectives and interests of participants in the ongoing political process rather than some external scientific or market-validated standard". p. 202.

3

THE UNITED STATES

* * *

A constant interplay among three propositions is discernible in how the United States has engaged with the idea of international order during its short history and in how its leaders continue to describe that engagement today: that material power is determinative; that law can shape and constrain behavior; and that the globalization of democracy decreases the likelihood of war. The anchor weight is the nation's sincere, enduring, and tightly held belief that liberty of expression, independence of action, and representation in the process by which constraints are placed on both is the best way to order internal politics. The centrifugal force is the extent to which the United States also believes that its security, and therefore the international order in which it exists, requires other states to share these convictions and to implement the political structures and processes their realization demands.

Power, Law, and Democracy

In the 5th century before the common era (BCE), ancient Greece's Plato produced what remains the conceptual wellspring of Western—which is to say European and North American—thinking about the ordering of human affairs.[1] Plato and his intellectual progeny were preoccupied primarily with individual comportment and its proper ordering through internal governance. The Greeks, Romans, and early Christians contemplated heaven and nature, working to uncover what they require of relations among humans and to reconcile them with human impulses and appetites. Although the task was to create political order, the work was to justify how doing so would enable each person to pursue her or his own version of a good life. Making political order benefit the individual, that is, was the locus of the inquiry, not the other way around.[2]

DOI: 10.4324/9781032723358-3

Broadly speaking, pre-modern Western paradigms concluded that it was only through a combination of cultivated reason, intentional self-realization, and the habits of ethical or, for religious theorists, divinely defined moral behavior that a social structure conducive to the pursuit of a good life could emerge. This emphasis on the responsibility and discipline required of a person, on one's duty and virtue—whether arrived at through reason or through religion—retained its power for centuries before becoming less central in the early modern period. By then, neither the cultivation of civic virtue nor of religious morality had proved particularly effective at preventing violence and discord, and the latter in fact had quite often been the cause of it.

By the 1600s, theories of social order based upon teachings of divine law were therefore being replaced by contractual theories based upon concepts of natural law. These theories not only retained each individual's pursuit of the good life as the objective of social order but also took natural equality as their starting assumption: all people were understood to be equally entitled to pursue a good life, just as they were equal in their instinct for self-preservation, in their desire to experience pleasure and to avoid pain, and in their responsiveness to self-interest. These impulses were not simply the human condition; as the products of natural law, they were the right and moral human condition. This meant that the problems of violence and discord could not be solved by morality because they were the outcome of it—of the inevitability that each individual's moral pursuit of the good life would conflict with that same pursuit by others.

With morality no longer accepted as a workable premise for social order, thinkers began instead to develop theories of consent and contract. These were derived from the idea that the drive for self-preservation and the desire to live a life defined more by fulfillment than by fear made it rational for individuals to cede a measure of liberty to an authority, a sovereign, empowered to enforce limitations on the pursuit of self-interest.

This proposition, that individuals have reason to accept constraints on their behavior, is the central, philosophical foundation of Western democracy. In practice, as a system of governance, Western democracy therefore operates through the application of three precepts: that the objective of politics is to enable individual pursuit of the good life; that individual consent to regulation of how one pursues the good life is given through the election of representatives; and that representatives define the substance and boundaries of sovereign authority.

Although writings during this early modern period generally remained obsessively focused on arriving at coherent arrangements of the ideas of consent and contract so as to structure civic life, and understandably so given the number, frequency, and brutality of the civil wars underway at the time, the same reasoning also began to infuse consideration of order in external affairs. By the middle of the 17th century, the intrusions of dueling religious empires into the workings of Europe's increasingly differentiated social units—nation-states, city-states, confederations, principalities, and so forth—had caused enough bloodshed to generate the 1648 Peace of Westphalia.[3] The simple wisdom of the attempt was to conclude that if violence is caused by dispute over which religious practice will order a society—if war, that is, is about who sets the rules and where—then it can be averted through a straightforward answer: *cuius regio, eius religio*: "whose realm, their religion". No religious empire, and no other ruler of territory however vast or small, in other words, was thereafter to seek the religious conversion of any population other than its own.

As the Peace of Westphalia, too, revealed itself to be an inadequate guarantor of orderly interstate relations, however, early ruminations on the applicability of ideas about authority and law to relations among nations began to appear. Three dominant propositions emerged about the force most capable of moderating international behavior: material power; law; and homogeneity of internal political systems, or system-unity. As does social contract theory, the ordering influence of each of these approaches relies upon the assumption of human rationality. In the context of external affairs, rationality presumes that leaders are responsive to costs and benefits and that their decisions are driven by the balance between the two. The three paradigms of external order differ, however, in how they understand the implications of that rationality.

The purported ordering influence of material power is captured neatly in the famous and oft-referenced axiom found in Thucydides' Melian dialogue, in which an Athenian delegation, confident in its might, reminds its less advantaged Melian interlocutors that in affairs of state the "strong do what they can and the weak suffer what they must".[4] Order for materialists, that is, is not achieved by design but rather by a natural sorting process, with the strong setting terms that allow them to achieve their interests expediently and with the weak exercising prudence by not objecting, or at least not objecting too strenuously.

It is from this precept that the large collection of modern Western theories of international relations that fall under the umbrella of realism emerges, a collection of theories that seek to explain how and why material power and variations in its distribution affect state behavior.[5] For realists, the order—the rules and behavioral expectations of international relations—changes only as does the distribution of power, whether that change is a reallocation of power from many states to few, or from few to many. Realism now includes many different and sizable subsets of ideas that, like siblings, share a core genetic material but differ in key characteristics and often fight with each other. Their differences notwithstanding, realist explanations for international order generally resemble each other in their association of the nature and type of that order with the nature and type of the powerful actors in it at any given time.

Not all historians and observers of political life, however, were or are convinced that it is power that is, or forever must be, determinative of order. To the contrary, there is an equally robust literature, liberal institutionalism, that is devoted to the idea that human constructs, law foremost among them, can shape and constrain interstate affairs.[6] For these thinkers, rational states, whether strong or weak, should seek to avoid war; fighting may bankrupt the loser, but it is expensive for the victor, too. Why, legalists ask, would rational states choose such a costly means of determining who will set the rules when a peaceful alternative is available? Even if the process of negotiating a legal regime is time consuming and requires compromise, after all, it is far preferable to the loss of life and damage to property that results from war.

While materialism is agnostic about, and legalism is at least accepting of, diversity in the form of governance internal to states, the third paradigm is neither. To the contrary, the system-unity paradigm, or democratic peace theory, directly connects representative forms of internal governance with orderly international behavior.[7] In addition to affirming the value of democracy in the first instance, its subsequent premise is that for human rationality to produce order, it must be the rationality of those who directly suffer the costs of disorder. Unaccountable authoritarian leaders do not. They don't pick up arms, and it's not their property that is destroyed or their prosperity that is immediately diminished when a war is fought. A true and durable international order can therefore only be the product of widespread republicanism. When all nations have representative forms of government, then all nations will choose means other than war to resolve disputes and set rules of acceptable conduct.

Over the course of its history, the United States has evidenced an impulse toward each of these theories, and sometimes toward more than one at a time. The country was formed during a period dominated by materialism, but the theory's core tenet—that might makes right—is discordant with the principles of representative democracy and consent upon which the United States is founded. The belief that achieving system-unity through the widespread adoption of liberal democracy will produce a lasting and durable peace has been a constant normative commitment and intellectual aspiration but only an occasional policy program. Legalism has split the difference, providing the nation with greater moral satisfaction than materialism, even if less than system-unity. Even this commitment to legalism, however, has been fickle, reflecting the internal contradictions of a country that wants simultaneously to be righteous and also to have its way.

The U.S. Relationship with the Post–War Order, 1945–2020

During America's first century, it took full advantage of the insulation provided by distance and water to firm up its hold on North America, to solidify its own internal politics, and to establish itself as an engine of commerce.[8] It was from this foundation that, around the time of its entry into its second century, it declared war on and quickly defeated Spain to contest that European nation's presence in Cuba, and then annexed Puerto Rico and the islands of Hawaii, Guam, and the Philippines. In the early 1900s, it further demonstrated its comfort with materialism as it flexed its naval power to take affairs in the Western hemisphere in hand and to prevent any other state from attempting the same—not just for purposes of security but also for purposes of securing the sea lanes necessary for interstate trade. It similarly extended itself into the waters of the Asia-Pacific, with President Teddy Roosevelt's Great White Fleet announcing to Japan, China, and Russia the resolve of the United States to prevent any one of them from running that region's affairs in full.

World War I, however, very quickly convinced many in the United States that continuation of this approach was simply not possible. The trouble was not only that the European continent's violent argument over which empire would control its middle was expressing itself in ways that ultimately caused America's entry as a belligerent but also that the system demonstrably was no longer capable of managing itself. The war—and in particular Germany's conduct in it, which included submarine attacks on naval vessels and private ships alike—galvanized U.S. involvement to protect the enablers of wealth-making trade: the absence of war among large and productive countries and accessible sea lanes through which commercial ships had safe passage to and from them.[9]

U.S. policymakers proposed to take on the nation's new responsibility in international affairs in a manner befitting their beliefs about America's identity as something apart from Europe. U.S. stewardship of order was therefore to be administrative, its involvement insulated from entanglement in distant feuds by the separation of juridical processes overseen by an international organization that would establish laws, mediate disputes, and enforce limitations where necessary.[10] This aspiration ultimately was a casualty of the conflict between a faction of Congressional isolationists and U.S. President Woodrow Wilson's unwillingness to compromise on his vision for the post-war peace.[11] The pursuit of a legalist world order, however, was resurrected with seriousness of purpose after World War II.

The Cold War

Having been shocked by the combustibility of Hitler's Nazism, the fear that fascism or other ideologies animated by the "philosophy of force" could overrun even the United States, or at least surround it, animated the U.S. approach to the post–war order. The U.N., which has been described as an American creation, its Charter as "fundamentally, an American document—conceived by Americans, negotiated by Americans, and made possible by Americans"—was designed to be a means through which ideologies unpalatable to the United States and its wartime allies would be corralled and wrestled into some form of submission.[12] The expectation was not that they would be wholly converted to a liberal economic and political model. The goal was instead that their edges would at least be softened or, if they were not, then confronted by an organized and powerful resistance.

At the time, U.S. occupation was reconfiguring German and Japanese politics, and so it was not a resurgence of prior grievances that was of concern. Even at that early date, it was Stalin's Soviet Union. The belief that communism was the new "philosophy of force" quickly captured the U.S. policymaking apparatus, enough so that within two years of the war's end, U.S. foreign policy already was expressly oriented around preventing Soviet expansionism and containing its influence.[13] First articulated in the 1947 Truman Doctrine, the objective of the U.S. strategy of containment was consistent with the orientation of the post–war order: it was not to create new democracies but rather to buffer those that already existed against Soviet intrusion and otherwise to prevent the spread of communism, especially if attempted through violence.[14] It was this concern that prompted the United States to enter its first peacetime alliance, the North Atlantic Treaty Organization (NATO).[15] The defense of liberal democracies against communist pressures was further reinforced by National Security Council Paper Number 68 (NSC68), presented to President Harry S. Truman in 1950.[16] NSC 68 made clear that containing communism would require a constant tending to U.S. military might. This meant the ongoing development of America's own capabilities, continuation of its presence in Europe and in Asia, and retaining, in aggregate, military advantage over the Soviet Union. U.S. military power thus became the backbone of the post–war order.

Containment of Soviet expansionism would be the defining characteristic of U.S. foreign policy for the four decades of Cold War that followed, placing different demands on the United States at different times—variations of perceived necessity that often were used to justify departures from the post–war order's core ideas, its institutions, and their rules. Although there were periods during which this divergence was pronounced, and periods during which the U.S. relationship with the institutions of the post–war order could be described less as maximally principled and more as minimally tolerant, the United States did not, between the order's founding and 2020, opt out. For different reasons at different times, U.S. presidential administrations instead chose to perpetuate the order they inherited rather than to make the order they wanted.

Early Conviction

In the brief period between World War II and the hardening of the Cold War, U.S. commitment to the nascent post–war order was strong, at least as it applied to the non-Soviet sphere of influence, which was very quickly subject to economic sanctions that significantly circumscribed trade. Most of these would stay in place for the duration of the next 50 years, with new restrictions added in response to events and in furtherance of the strategic goals of various presidential administrations.

During this early period, the policies that support for free-trade multilateralism necessitated were determined more by the need to address problems of the recent past than by the opportunity to plan for the coming future. During their first decade, the IMF and World Bank were relatively quiescent, as the United States funded European reconstruction directly through the Marshall Plan and Japanese reconstruction through occupation. Both efforts accepted that rebuilding these national economies would include discriminatory measures that might adversely affect U.S. industry for some period of time, believing that this was justified by the need to consolidate an economically stable non-communist block.

Latency in the order's financial institutions persisted into the 1960s, during which decade the IMF's role in international politics has been described as "episodic, and from a global perspective minor", with its "value derived primarily from its passive embodiment of the understandings and commitments" of the Bretton Woods system.[17] In the 1970s, its major preoccupation was adjusting to the effects of the U.S. decision to sever the dollar from gold and defining its role in the new floating-rate regime. The World Bank spent these decades concentrating on financing infrastructure, supporting agriculture, and cultivating industrialization in developing countries. Both institutions operated largely in the background of U.S. politics and policy, with the government making and adjusting its contributions as negotiated by the technocrats charged with managing U.S. institutional interests.

The U.N. by comparison was far from idle. To the contrary, it and the U.S. commitment to it were tested in short order. First came the Soviet blockade of Berlin in 1948, to which the Truman administration responded by airlift and by referral to the U.N. for resolution.[18] That referral, according to Dean Rusk, who at the time was the director of the Office of United Nations Affairs, was not "just to make a record but in the hope of getting a settlement"—even if that settlement was not to U.S. liking.[19]

Similarly in 1950, when North Korea invaded South Korea, the Truman administration responded by sponsoring a police action under U.N. auspices and coordinated its military efforts with the 16 member states contributing to the effort. Truman chose to act, first and foremost to forestall a communist advance, but he chose to do it in a way that would also demonstrate that the U.N. was not already a dead letter.[20] When U.S. General Douglas McArthur exceeded his authority as commander of those U.N. forces, crossing the 38th parallel despite its risk of provoking China's entry into the war and without President Truman's approval, he was removed from command in part—though not in full—to assuage unhappy members of the U.N. coalition. The United States, moreover, acceded to a termination of the conflict without having achieved a conclusive end in order "to maintain the maximum degree of United Nations unity in Korea", a decision interpreted as "evidence of American intent to make collective security work" through the United Nations.[21]

Truman's successor, President Dwight D. Eisenhower, was expressive in his support for the United Nations, asserting that the United States "shall work with all others—especially through this great organization, the United Nations—so that peaceful and reasonable negotiations may replace the clash of the battlefield".[22] In 1953 Eisenhower delivered a speech to the General Assembly in which he recounted the extent of U.S. nuclear capability, acknowledged Soviet possession of its own arsenal, and used both facts to entreat member states not only to seek "the reduction or elimination of atomic materials available for military purposes" but also to seek means of using atomic energy for "peaceful power".[23] The address, referred to as the "Atoms for Peace" speech, is credited as being the genesis of the U.N. International Atomic Energy

Agency (IAEA). Eisenhower also engaged the United States, through the United Nations, in "peaceful and reasonable" negotiations of a nuclear non-proliferation regime. These negotiations in 1968 culminated in the international Treaty on the Nonproliferation of Nuclear Weapons (NPT).

U.S. foreign policy on the whole, however, in the words of one contemporary analyst, evidenced much "inconstancy" in its relationship with the U.N. and largely was "destined . . . in the immediate future to support the United Nations only in crises, but as in the past, to forget how valuable it can be between crises".[24] Over time, moreover, interest transitioned from considering whether and how the strategic objective of containing the Soviet Union could strengthen the post–war order's ability to keep peace to a preoccupation with whether and how the institutions of the post–war order could serve the U.S. strategic objectives of weakening the Soviet Union and blocking the spread of communism.[25] By the end of the Eisenhower administration, it was clear to one observer that the United Nations "was captured by the cold war, and was transformed into an instrument of policy in the American struggle against the Communist World".[26]

The tendency to look to the U.N. during periods of crises and to use it as a tool through which to fight communism continued into and through the Kennedy and Johnson administrations. Kennedy thus proffered a moving remembrance of the recently deceased U.N. Secretary General Dag Hammarskjold, intoning that "in the development of this organization rests the only true alternative to war". He also initiated a small Military Assistance Command to support the government of South Vietnam, then in conflict with communist forces in the North—an action that he addressed at the U.N. but for which he did not seek that body's approval. As that war escalated both his administration and the Johnson administration that followed Kennedy's assassination in 1962 did repeatedly, and fruitlessly, express interest in a U.N.-managed negotiation process through which to find "an acceptable formula to restore peace and security in Indo-China".[27] Kennedy had not, however, done similarly with either the second Berlin Crisis (1961) or the Cuban Missile Crisis (1962), both of which the administration instead handled unilaterally and with threats of force.[28]

Growing Instrumentalism

The attitude of the Nixon administration that followed was colored by perceptions of the U.N.'s fecklessness during the preceding decade and by the temperaments and philosophies of the president and his key advisers. Nixon in particular had a general distaste for the U.N. and the administration's primary preoccupations were attending to domestic politics and to the U.S. position vis à vis the Soviet Union.[29] Their interest in the U.N. and in the other post-war institutions thus varied with their belief that those institutions were useful instruments for shining Nixon's image at home or for blocking, balancing, or surpassing Soviet achievements and the spread of communism abroad.[30]

These motivations were most visible in the decision to break the Bretton Woods financial regime in 1971—done to defend the U.S. dollar without degrading Nixon's chance at reelection—and in the administration's maneuvering to supplant Taiwan with the PRC at the U.N. that same year. The latter was poorly received within the United States, causing an upsurge in negative sentiment among the U.S. population and bringing Senator Barry Goldwater to fume that

> the time has come for us to cut off all financial help, withdraw as a member, and ask the United Nations to find a headquarters location outside of the United States that is more in keeping with the philosophy of the majority of voting members, some place like Moscow or Peking.[31]

This criticism proved an ineffective deterrent to the Nixon administration's continued outreach to China, which it pursued opportunistically as a means of drawing Beijing away from the Soviet Union.[32] Over the remainder of Nixon's term, and throughout that of his successor Gerald Ford and of Ford's successor Jimmy Carter, this effort included repeated high-level diplomatic contacts and carefully calibrated inducements for China to move toward participation in the global economy. The outcome was two formal communiques, the term of art for statements of understanding and intent on key issues of bilateral concern. The first communique established the foundational terms of U.S. involvement in the dispute over Taiwan's status, which was then solidified in the second communique.

Together, the two communiques defined the U.S. position on the Taiwan question as acknowledging the disagreement between the two and taking sides with neither, so long as neither used force to settle the matter. In practical terms, this meant that Taiwan was not unilaterally to declare formal independence—because the PRC was clear and unequivocal in its position that doing so would impel it to go to war to win control of the island—and that the United States would ensure that China had incentive not to try to do so simply because the China-Taiwan military balance indicated that it could. Toward this end, the second communique was accompanied by the U.S. Taiwan Relations Act (TRA), a piece of Congressional legislation that decreed the United States would be militarily prepared to come to the defense of Taiwan if needed and that it would sell Taiwan "defense articles and defense services in such quantity as may be necessary to enable Taiwan to maintain a sufficient self-defense capability".[33] In 1982, the two communiques were joined with a third, in which the United States indicated it would moderate its level of arms sales consistent with changes in PRC military capabilities. This third communique was then joined by the Six Assurances, which the United States issued to reassure Taiwan that it would not let the PRC dictate the terms of U.S. military support and that the United States would never pressure Taipei to into negotiations with Beijing.[34] This collection of issuances and agreements—the three communiques, the TRA, and the Six Assurances—were skillfully managed over the next four decades as the "One-China Policy". It was the second communique, signed under the administration of President Jimmy Carter in 1979, that initiated mutual recognition and thereby officially normalized the U.S.-China relationship. The United States also extended most favored nation trading status to China that year, although China was not a member of the GATT.

The Nixon and, after his resignation, the Ford administrations treated free trade with a similar strategic-mindedness. Nixon used reduction of sanctions on members of the Soviet bloc to try to splinter it and as a means of inducing Soviet cooperation during the thaw in relations of the early 1970s.[35] During Ford's term, the economic picture was particularly complicated, with an oil embargo imposed by Arab producers and a price hike effected by the Organization of Petroleum Exporting Countries (OPEC). Although it ultimately did not do so, the Ford administration considered using restrictions on the export of food and grain to try to exert leverage against OPEC. So too did its response to dissatisfaction from developing nations about the inequities of the international economic system demonstrate less a belief in any orthodoxy about the role of the post–war order in generating global wealth than a fixation on defending and promoting U.S. interests.[36]

President Jimmy Carter arrived with a different mindset, entering office having campaigned on the promise of implementing a new "world order politics" that would more directly prioritize liberal principles and values. On the agenda were nuclear disarmament and a reduction in military spending, investment in global development, and advancing human rights.

Carter's interest in human rights was genuine, focused, and very quickly infused into his administration's policies and operations. At the outset of his term, the State Department developed a strategy for promoting human rights, established a policy coordination committee, and "set out general principles to be followed and a series of questions to be used in determining if there were violations of internationally recognized human rights as defined by the United Nations Universal Declaration of Human Rights of 1948". So too did Carter convey to the international community the direction his administration would take on the role of human rights in U.S. foreign policy, informing the assembled members of the U.N., in his first speech to that body, that none "can claim that mistreatment of its citizens is solely its own business".[37]

Far from being a rigid construct, however, the administration's approach to making human rights an important feature of its relationships with other states was not dogmatic or punitive. To the contrary, Carter preferred appeals and inducements to threats and sanctions, and so policy was designed to "consider the nature and extent of the violations in a particular country, the 'level of political development' in that nation, and the 'direction of human rights trend[s] there'".[38] The goal, moreover, was the gradual "enhancement of basic human rights in diverse societies". The Carter administration did not "seek to change governments" or to "remake other countries in the image of the United States".[39] So too was the administration realistic and pragmatic about the tradeoffs that would sometimes be necessary, acknowledging "that there were 'other major objectives of U.S. foreign policy that are of equal—and in some situations greater—importance' than human rights".[40]

Such tradeoffs did, indeed, characterize Carter's four years in office. Despite early optimism, Carter relatively quickly concluded that the prospect of developing a more cooperative relationship with the Soviet Union was low, as was the probability of any improvement in its human rights record.[41] These assessments encouraged the administration's cultivation of China. Although Carter was hopeful that normalization would "lead to a gradual improvement of China's human rights", his administration did not make this either a prerequisite or even a prominent feature of that process.[42] For Carter, the Soviet invasion of Afghanistan in 1979 solidified and validated the fact and the manner of this approach.[43] It also led his administration to reorient U.S. policy around limiting Soviet influence in the developing world, produced a pledge to increase the U.S. defense budget by 3%, and resulted in the imposition of unilateral diplomatic and economic sanctions.[44] In so doing, Carter presaged an anti-communist activism in U.S. foreign policy that would continue into and through the two terms of the administration of President Ronald Reagan.

Late-Phase Activism

The Reagan administration's strategy for prevailing in the U.S.-Soviet rivalry was itself in many ways in contradiction to, if not outright contravention of, the post–war order's animating ideas and institutions.[45] Reagan demonstrated no compunction about elevating the role of force in U.S. foreign policy. His administration oversaw a considerable increase in U.S. defense spending, which, though always a pillar of containment, had varied in magnitude and emphasis over time. This largesse in funding, the pursuit of "peace through strength", would leave the United States with a surfeit of military capability at the Cold War's end, ushering in a period of unmatched U.S. military primacy.[46]

The second of Reagan's legacies was an activist implementation of the containment strategy, one that extended beyond Carter's elevation of human rights to include an overt emphasis on democratization. Since its introduction under Truman, the objective of containment was not to create new democracies but rather to buffer those that already existed against Soviet intrusion and otherwise to prevent the spread of communism.[47] The approach, reinforced by NSC68, was to encourage democratization by example and inducement and to protect extant democracies—and nascent ones, as had been the case in the Republic of Korea in 1950—against communist threats.[48] The Reagan Doctrine, however, was a "full-court-press" with a program for democratization and public declarations of "American support for anticommunist revolution 'on every continent from Afghanistan to Nicaragua'".[49]

The democratization agenda of the Reagan Doctrine thus broke from NSC68's pragmatic argument that "in relations between nations, the prime reliance of the free society is on the strength and appeal of its idea and it feels no compulsion sooner or later to bring all societies into conformity with it".[50] So too did some of its democratization activities—the invasion of Grenada in 1983, for example, and its trade embargo of Nicaragua and covert support for a group working to overthrow the government there—violate the U.N. Charter's prohibition on intervention in the internal affairs of other sovereign states.[51]

Reagan's personal regard for the United Nations itself, however, did travel some distance during his two terms. He entered office having described the organization in ways that made it seem an irrelevant nuisance. He is quoted, for example, as having argued that the United States need not be "bound by the votes of the U.N., because it is a debating society".[52] Once in office his White House took a notably harsh stance, cutting off funding to various U.N. entities, withdrawing U.S. participation from others, and making it known that there would be rewards for members with a pro-U.S. voting record and penalties for the converse.[53] As events continued to accumulate, however, Reagan came to see at least tactical value in the U.N. He used it as a platform upon which to credibly make overtures for cooperation with Moscow and found it helpful in addressing a number of regional problems and crises. By the end of his term, Reagan was outwardly appreciative of the U.N.'s performance in these instances and congratulatory of what he deemed its progress in making reforms that made it a more useful tool in international politics.[54]

Reagan's full court press also affected U.S. economic policy and the post–war order's economic institutions. In 1983, the administration issued National Security Decision Directive 75, in which it was determined that the United States, without consultation with its allies and partners, would impose additional trade sanctions on the Soviet Union.[55] It was also in the 1980s that the extent and type of conditions attached to IMF and World Bank Loans underwent a substantial change. In a break from prior practice, the two institutions shifted from dispensing funds with traditional banking conditions attached to making loans contingent on the recipient government's willingness to liberalize its economy. These conditions, it turned out, were applied with greater frequency to countries perceived to be at risk of adopting communism.[56] Requirements for domestic policy changes thus were regularly attached to loans given to countries in Latin America, the Middle East, and Sub-Saharan Africa.[57]

The Reagan Doctrine was not, however, an expression of a directed, focused effort to construct a democratic peace. Reagan's marriage of military might with democratic agitation was, rather, a response to what it understood to be the demands of containing communism, confronting the Soviet Union, and the imperatives of U.S. domestic politics.[58] Nonetheless, it did bring democratization explicitly into the fore of U.S. foreign policy. This legacy endured in the language of the administrations that followed Reagan and the 1991 collapse of the Soviet Union, and in some cases also featured very prominently in their actions.

After the Cold War

Three of the five post–Cold War presidential administrations, those of George H.W. Bush, William J. Clinton, and Barack Obama, regularly used the language of universal rights and democratization, but in action hewed more closely to the precepts and institutions of the legalist post–war order. The first of the post–Cold War presidents, George H.W. Bush was committed to market liberalization and to supporting burgeoning democracies, though not at the expense of the post-war institutions.

Indeed, and despite its association with the idea of "a new world order", the H.W. Bush administration was comparatively quite diligent in supporting the old one.

Narratively, the 1990s started with rhetorical flourish (in sentiment if not in delivery) as President George H.W. Bush invited the world to understand the collapse of the Soviet Union as an opportunity for a "new world order". Undergirded by the steadying, and militarily powerful, hand of the United States, this new order would propagate liberal ideals—sovereign self-determination, democracy, human rights, and economic exchange. Over the subsequent decade, however, the contours of international political life were discussed in far less evocative terms, focusing not on the global project of liberal order but rather on the extent and durability of U.S. primacy.[59] These ideas may have been considered by many to be related, but they were not at the time understood to be the same.[60]

Bush, himself a former Ambassador to the United Nations, was a committed multilateralist—although not a dogmatic one, as the 1989 U.S. intervention in Panama, without U.N. approval, made clear—and generally sought to reinforce the role of the U.N. in ordering international politics. He was an advocate of upholding the dictates of the U.N. Charter, which he largely did in word and in deed, most visibly so by working through the U.N. to galvanize a multilateral military response to the 1991 Iraqi invasion of Kuwait.[61] H.W. Bush described the significance of this event and the manner of the organized international response to it in legalist terms, as an effort to secure "not simply our energy or economic security and the stability of a vital region but the prospects for peace in the post–Cold war era—the promise of a new world order based upon the rule of law".[62] According to his national security advisor Brent Scowcroft, the "new" part of the world order was in designing and demonstrating coalition building for collective action, one that featured major power cooperation and thus was "a model for dealing with future crises in the post–Cold War world . . . a model for dealing with aggressors. The U.S. should behave in a way that others can trust and get U.N. support".[63] Bush's policies regarding the secessionist violence in Yugoslavia and the warlord-induced violence in Somalia in the early 1990s were consistent with this orientation. In both cases, the Bush administration joined U.N. efforts at mediation and peacekeeping rather than taking unilateral action or working through the NATO alliance.

Bush was also committed to free trade, to an extent that was to his own domestic political detriment. He insisted on maintaining China's most-favored-nation status after the Chinese Communist Party's brutal reaction to pro-democracy protests in 1989 and was willing to impose only a limited sanctions regime which—along with the decision to send high-level representatives to Beijing one month after the event—was roundly criticized as being an unjustifiably mild rebuke.[64] Bush also was unwilling to play economic hardball with Japan and Europe on issues like car exports and market access. He did, however, successfully bring the leaders of Canada and Mexico to sign the North American Free Trade Agreement (NAFTA) regional trading bloc, though ratification was left to the next administration.

The successor to the Bush administration's single term, President Bill Clinton, entered office much less interested in attaching his administration's policies to any particular idea of global order than he was in associating it with economic prosperity. Because he was convinced that domestic prosperity required international prosperity and that both furthered the appeal of democracy which in turn furthered the likelihood of system-unity's promise of long-term international peace and stability, his administration's preferred foreign policy agenda was economics- and diplomacy-forward.[65] North Korea's nuclear weapons program and political violence in Haiti, Rwanda, and the Balkans, however, relatively quickly forced an otherwise disinclined administration to wrestle with particularly vexing questions about the value, utility, and limitations of the post–war order in the post-Soviet world.

When justifying a U.S. military response to the violent and non-democratic behaviors of General Raoul Cedras and his junta in Haiti in 1994, Clinton managed simultaneously to express his reluctance for the United States to be the guarantor of the post–war order and also his desire for the United States to retain credibility as the primary defender of liberal values.[66] He did similarly as he sought to explain U.S. intervention after the dissolution of Yugoslavia, which precipitated a period of pronounced violence that over time became an organized campaign of ethnic cleansing in which Serbs expelled and murdered Bosnian Muslims. In this instance the Clinton administration worked with the United Nations and NATO to implement an arms embargo and a no-fly zone, to create and defend safe-havens, to execute a bombing campaign, and to deploy peacekeeping forces.[67] Clinton caveated these multilateral engagements, however, with the assurance that they would go only so far; the United States would never "subcontract" its foreign policy to another entity.[68]

The Clinton administration was equally in a vise when it came to trade relations. Clinton was a committed free-trader who assumed office during a period in which popular sentiment, shaped by the economic recession of the late 1980s, was turning against it. He nonetheless shepherded NAFTA through the ratification process, and it was during his first term, in 1995, that the GATT transformed into the World Trade Organization. It was at the end of his second term, in 2001, that China formally entered.

The U.S. relationship with the post-war financial institutions was by comparison more fraught. The IMF in particular faced skepticism about its continued value in the post–Cold War world as a recalcitrant Congress delayed and debated the merits of replenishing the IMF's dwindling resources in the aftermath of the 1997 East Asian Financial Crisis, though it did finally do so.[69] The Clinton years thus were neither/nor: the goal was not to hasten the arrival of a widespread democratic peace, the administration's policies did not consistently affirm the tenets of the legalist, free-trade multilateralist, post–war order, and neither did they consistently undermine them.

The foreign policy agenda of George W. Bush, by comparison, was radical. Bush's "freedom agenda" was the policy expression of the administration's conclusion, arrived upon after the terrorist attacks of 9/11, that America's security "increasingly depends on the success of liberty in other lands", and that "the fundamental character of regimes now matters more than the international distribution of power".[70]

At a level of principle, U.S. foreign policy under W. Bush was not protective of the post–war order. The United States embedded autonomy and activism in its strategy documents.[71] Its pursuit of a system-unity order, a democratic peace, made internal political conversion of other states a valid objective of U.S. national security strategy, and it invaded Afghanistan and Iraq with the express project of interfering in their internal affairs.[72] Despite the troubled progression and poor results of both efforts, which were apparent by the end of the administration's second term, President Bush signed National Security Presidential Directive (NSPD) 58 before departing office in 2008. NSPD58 was entitled "Institutionalizing the Freedom Agenda: President Bush Calls on Future Presidents and Congresses to Continue Leading the Cause of Freedom Worldwide". The document was forwarded by way of reminding future leaders that "the advancement of freedom is the most effective long-term measure for strengthening international stability, reducing regional conflicts, countering terrorism and terror-supporting extremists, and extending peace and prosperity" and to offer them a prescriptive, action-specific "blueprint" for promoting "democracy and freedom systematically".[73]

At the level of practice, however, the W. Bush administration's record is far from destructive of the post–war order. It expanded foreign aid if not through, then at least alongside, the post-war financial institutions.[74]

Although it "could not avoid the use of protectionist measures at home" it was a vocal supporter of free trade and entered into bilateral and multilateral trade deals.[75] Despite assuming office skeptical of the IMF and World Bank, the administration's posture softened over time as it came to view the institutions as "key mechanisms for advancing its foreign economic policies".[76] This pattern was equally evident in the administration's relationship with the United Nations, where an early period of ambivalence evolved into an active and effective working relationship after the terrorist attacks of 9/11. Respected ambassadors with access to the President represented the White House, President Bush consistently delivered a speech at the opening session of each General Assembly, and he cultivated relationships with two consecutive Secretaries General. W. Bush's use of the United Nations, intended to further U.S. interests, thus "ironically, strengthened the body's long-term and immediate role in global affairs", even as it did not reflect a fundamental recommitment to the principles of the post–war order.[77]

President Barack Obama did not take up his predecessor's call to "Continue Leading the Cause of Freedom Worldwide"—because of his own disinclination toward democratization, because he understood the electorate to be dissatisfied with Bush's post-9/11 interventionism and state-building projects, and because of the circumstances under which he assumed office. Obama's two terms were instead consumed with managing the policy problems caused by events and non-events the administration either had inherited, or over which it had limited control, and sometimes both: the denouement of the war in Iraq, an inability to achieve the same in Afghanistan, and the 2008 global financial crisis. While the wars were largely U.S. problems with U.S. solutions, the financial crisis was not. Recognizing that neither it, nor any other state, could singularly address its effects, the Obama administration worked multilaterally to infuse the IMF with funds for emergency response in the short term and to design mechanisms through which to prevent a repeat occurrence in the long term.[78]

While grappling with these and other events, the administration was certainly willing to extol the virtues of human rights and democracy, but it did so while also working narratively and in action to temper perceptions of U.S. exceptionalism. Obama's speeches frequently referenced the need for America to refine and improve its own democratic practices and to better realize liberal principles and human rights. He acknowledged past foreign policy missteps and overreaches and voiced belief in the promise of multilateralism.[79] In policy Obama sought to advance free trade, most notably through the large and inclusive Trans-Pacific Partnership Agreement, a strategic free trade initiative that would bind the United States and many of its allies and partners into closer economic relationships with the countries of East Asia. He also worked to advance climate cooperation, to minimize the use of force in international politics, and to affirm the centrality of the United Nations.[80]

When confronted in 2012 with evidence that Syrian President Bashar Assad was using chemical weapons against his own population, for example, Obama first threatened to use force to compel him to stop but ultimately pursued a negotiated agreement, backed by a U.N. Security Council resolution, for the weapons' destruction.[81] Obama similarly responded to Russia's territorial aggression against Ukraine not with force, but with firm diplomacy and economic sanctions. And in 2015, the administration, together with the other permanent members of the U.N. security council and Germany, completed an agreement with Iran to reduce the international security risks of its nuclear program. Thus although the administration regularly asserted the value of and its support for human rights and democracy worldwide, it also pursued a policy agenda that positioned the United States as being committed to free-trade multilateralism and as a central stakeholder of the post–war order.

The administration of Donald J. Trump, too, was disinterested in democratization, though it also was disinterested in free-trade and in multilateralism. Trump renounced virtually every fundamental tenet of foreign policy that the United States had pursued since World War II. Under the banner of seeking to make America "great again" by putting "America first", Trump's foreign policy was wholly materialist and militarized. Trump was not simply dismissive of the post-war institutions but disdainful of them, most especially of the United Nations, which he described as weak, incompetent, and "not a friend of democracy . . . not a friend to freedom . . . not even to the United States of America where, as you know, it has its home".[82] Unlike Reagan and George W. Bush, there was no evolution of this position over the course of Trump's four-year term. He was unrepentant about breaking the Trans-Pacific Partnership (TPP) and unabashedly self-satisfied about engaging in a trade war with China that did not, as had been the justification, solve America's trade deficit but instead harmed the U.S. economy.[83]

So too was Trump not just willing but in fact eager to capitalize upon or to create opportunities to threaten use of U.S. military might, threats that despite Trump's own alleged opposition to nuclear weapons occasionally invoked the possibility of using them.[84] The administration's National Defense Strategy (NDS) focused the attention of the Department of Defense squarely on modernization—code for investing in high-technology warfighting capabilities—in preparation for a "high-end conflict" with a "near-peer", with China as the unnamed nearest-peer. Insofar as the Trump administration can be said to have had a coherent worldview, much less a preference for world order, then its dimensions were only two: that the United States should be free to pursue its interests as it sees fit, where, when, and how it sees fit; and that for this to be true, the errors in U.S. economic and foreign policy, most especially the free-trade multilateralism that had allowed China to become an economic and military competitor of the United States, must be corrected and U.S. dominance in both domains restored. To the extent that Trump himself was a vehicle through which segments of the U.S. population could mobilize their own discontents and preferences, his presidency suggested that the nation's attachment to the post–war order was becoming tenuous from the bottom up, not just the top down.[85]

The U.S. Record of Compliance and Defiance

Despite its role in the establishment of the post–war order, the United States thereafter vacillated between full-throated endorsement of its principles and its institutions, equivocation about America's willingness to assume the obligations and duties of its membership in them, and loud objections to the notion of being constrained by their rules.[86] Variation over time is explainable at least partly by differences in policymaker worldviews and priorities, and yet partly it is not. Even those U.S. leaders who were vocal and believably sincere in their support of the post–war order and its institutions introduced policies that were contrary to them and that stretched, bent, and sometimes broke their rules. Whatever the specific reasons and rationales motivating divergence in the moment, taken over time, the United States was an inconstant gardener of the principles of the post–war order and of its institutions.

The United States, for example, negotiated and ratified a network of multilateral and bilateral arms control treaties—some negotiated through the United Nations and others outside it—designed to restrict and manage the development, possession, placement, and use of weapons of mass destruction and conventional military assets.[87] It also, however, has declined to be party to numerous other U.N. treaties, many of which are notable for the issues they address, for the number of other states that are party to them, and in some cases for the extent to which U.S. refusal seems inconsistent with its own espoused values and principles.[88] As described by one expert,

> The United States constantly fails to sign or ratify treaties the rest of the world supports. It has failed to ratify treaties that tackle

biodiversity and greenhouse gas emissions, protect the rights of children and women, and govern international waters. . . . In fact, the United States has one of the worst records of any country in ratifying human rights and environmental treaties.[89]

It often is argued that U.S. refusal to sign many of the multilateral treaties and conventions produced by the U.N. is offset by its practice of abiding by their terms. Conceptually this may be a satisfying answer. Practically, the U.S. unwillingness to treat its own preferred norms as rules—and to refuse to do so because it doesn't want to be susceptible to charges of noncompliance and because accession might impinge upon U.S. sovereignty—is a confusing and, increasingly, an untenable position for a nation professing the necessity of, and its own determination to, uphold the post–war order.

During the Cold War, U.S. policymakers prioritized the nation's rivalry with the Soviet Union. Their efforts to prevent the spread of communism meant that the United States was at turns an enabler and an impediment to the United Nations, and to the institution's efforts to act in service of international security. After the Cold War, the United States had and exercised more latitude in galvanizing U.N. action, but it did so inconsistently. In the 1990s, it led the U.N. response to Iraq's breach of Kuwaiti sovereignty, worked with the U.N. to monitor and maintain a ceasefire among warring factions in Somalia, participated in U.N. operations and peacekeeping activities in the Balkans, and ultimately, sought U.N. approval before engaging NATO forces in that conflict. And although the United States was long the largest contributor to the U.N.'s regular budget, a 1994 Congressional cap put the United States chronically in arrears thereafter in its mandatory contributions to the U.N. peacekeeping budget.[90]

So too did the United States covertly intervene in and invade other countries—Vietnam (1964–1973), Grenada (1983), Panama (1989), and Iraq (2003)—without U.N. approval and indeed despite its denunciation. These wars were not for purposes of territorial acquisition, but they were for purposes of ideological emplacement and, in some instances, regime overthrow, objectives that defy the U.N. Charter's prohibition on interfering with the internal affairs of other states. They also contributed to the expansion of U.S. military presence worldwide. At the end of 2020, the United States had more than 700 bases—some large and permanent, others very small and mobile—in 80 countries.[91] The U.S. defense budget was $331 billion in 2001 and $778 billion in 2020, with a nuclear arsenal of approximately 3,800 nuclear warheads ready for delivery by 800 ballistic missiles and aircraft.[92]

The U.S. record of compliance with and support for the post-war financial institutions is similarly mixed. Although it unilaterally ended the Bretton Woods exchange rate regime and there were sporadic calls for the United States to extricate itself from the post-war financial institutions altogether, this position never gained enough traction to produce withdrawal. It instead continuously provided financial support for the operations of the IMF and World Bank but without any consistent vigor in otherwise expressing its commitment to their stewardship.

In matters of free trade, the United States was a named respondent in 39 of 133 total GATT disputes—claims by other members of the treaty that the United States was in violation of its terms—and was the state most frequently charged, by a wide range of countries, with breaking the WTO's rules.[93] It also was the state most frequently found to be in violation of those rules, receiving more adverse judgments from the institution's Dispute Settlement Board (DSB) than any other member, losing 90% of the claims brought against it.[94] The United States was a ready participant in U.N. sanctions regimes and was quite comfortable imposing them unilaterally—which it did most often for purposes of pressuring others into alignment with its own policy priorities and not to demand anyone else's compliance with institutional rules.[95] In the 44 years between 1946 and 1990, the United States initiated at least 191 sanctions on 74 states; in the 27 years between 1991 and 2018, those numbers increased to 252 sanctions on 101 states.[96]

Despite this record, the United States throughout maintained an unflagging perception of itself as the leader of the post–war order and not as a hegemon pursuing its own material interests and using military power to promote its preferred liberal values. Indeed, the Biden administration repeatedly made the case that continued U.S. leadership of the post–war order was necessary to prevent "movement away from the universal values that have sustained so much of the world's progress over the past 75 years" and toward "one governed by brute force".[97]

Today, China is seeking to puncture if not America's own belief in this portrayal, then certainly that of others. And while perfection in past adherence to or enforcement of the post–war order's principles and institutional rules is not a meaningful standard, perceptions of performance have taken on a new significance as the United States and China both seek to distinguish their behaviors and burnish their credentials with audiences worldwide.

* * *

Notes

1 Michael Curtis, Ed., *The Great Political Theories, Volume 1* (New York: Avon Books), 1961; Simon Leys, "An Introduction to Confucius", in Simon Leys, Ed., *The Hall of Uselessness: Collected Essays* (New York: NYRB), 2011, pp. 314–328.
2 For the Christians, the primary concern was with the soul—one per person, all with equal standing before God. Devotion to the political structures into which one was born was expected, as both the timing of one's existence and the political structures of that time were determined by God, and the structure's purpose was to allow individuals to behave in ways that prepared their souls for the afterlife.
3 The Peace of Westphalia is a "peace" and not a "treaty" because it is not codified in a single document. It is, rather, a tripartite grouping of agreements: the Peace of Munster; the Treaty of Munster; and the Treaty of Osnabruck. Ove Bring, "The Westphalian Peace Tradition in International Law: From *Jus ad Bellum to Jus contra Bellum*", *International Law Studies*, Vol. 75, 2000, pp. 58–80, https://digital-commons.usnwc.edu/cgi/viewcontent.cgi?article=1435&context=ils.
4 Thucydides, *History of the Peloponnesian War* (London: Penguin Classics), 1963.
5 Classic realist texts include: Hans Morgenthau, *Politics among Nations: The Struggle for Power and Peace* (New York: Knopf), 1967; E. H. Carr, *The Twenty Years' Crisis, 1919–1939* (New York: Macmillan Company), 1939; Kenneth Waltz, *Theory of International Politics* (Reading, MA: Addison-Wesley), 1979; and more recently, John Mearsheimer, *The Tragedy of Great Power Politics* (New York: WW Norton), 2014. For a critical review of the tenets of realism, see: Jeffrey W. Legro and Andrew Moravcsik, "Is Anybody Still a Realist?", *International Security*, Vol. 24, No. 2, Fall 1999, pp. 5–55.
6 Claire Cutler, "The 'Grotian Tradition' in International Relations", *Review of International Studies*, Vol. 17, No. 1, 1991, pp. 41–65; Robert O. Keohane and Lisa L. Martin, "The Promise of Institutionalist Theory", *International Security*, Vol. 20, No. 1, 1995, pp. 39–51.
7 R. Burles, "Kant's Domestic Analogy: International and Global Order", *European Journal of International Relations*, Vol. 29, No. 2, 2023, pp. 501–522. https://doi.org/10.1177/13540661221133976; Michael W. Doyle, "Liberalism and World Politics", *The American Political Science Review*, Vol. 80, No. 4, December 1986, pp. 1151–1169, www.jstor.org/stable/pdf/1960861.pdf?refreqid=exc elsior%3Ac0280ce5acb438286639fe5cc6cc277b&ab_segments=& origin=&initiator=.
8 Charles A. Kupchan, *Isolationism: A History of America's Efforts to Shield Itself from the World* (New York: Oxford University Press), 2020.

9 David Fromkin, *In the Time of the Americans* (New York: Vintage Books), 1995, pp. 144–194; Robert Kagan, *Ghost at the Feast: America and the Collapse of World Order, 1900–1941* (New York: Knopf), 2023, pp. 126, 184–185, 189–191.

10 David Fromkin, *In the Time of the Americans*, pp. 260–282; Charles Kupchan, *Isolationism*, pp. 233–235, 253–254; Robert Kagan, *The Ghost at the Feast*, pp. 227–243.

11 Charles Kupchan, *Isolationism*, pp. 252–253; David Fromkin, *In the Time of the Americans*, pp. 350–354; "Joint Declaration by the President of the United States of America and Mr. Winston Churchill, Representing His Majesty's Government in the United Kingdom, Known as the Atlantic Charter", August 14, 1941.

12 Oona A. Hathaway and Scott J. Shapiro, *The Internationalists: How a Radical Plan to Outlaw War Remade the World* (New York: Simon & Schuster Paperbacks), 2017, p. 213.

13 Robert L. Messer, "Paths not Taken: The United States Department of State and Alternatives to Containment, 1945–46", *Diplomatic History*, Vol. 1, No. 4, 1977, pp. 297–319; "Aid to Greece and Turkey: The Truman Doctrine", March 12, 1947, https://usa.usembassy.de/etexts/speeches/rhetoric/hstaid.htm.

14 "Aid to Greece and Turkey".

15 Lawrence S. Kaplan, *Origins of NATO: 1948–1949*, 34 EMORY INT'L L. REV. 11, 2019, https://scholarlycommons.law.emory.edu/eilr/vol34/iss0/2.

16 As written in NSC68, the report presented to President Harry S. Truman in 1950, which set the direction of U.S. national security policy in the Cold War:

The absence of order among nations is becoming less and less tolerable. This fact imposes on us, in our own interests, the responsibility of world leadership. It demands that we make the attempt, and accept the risks inherent in it, to bring about order and justice by means consistent with the principles of freedom and democracy.

"NSC 68: United States Objectives and Programs for National Security", April 14, 1950; Louis W. Koenig, "The Truman Doctrine and NATO", *Current History*, Vol. 57, No. 335, 1969, pp. 18–53, www.jstor.org/stable/45312128.

17 James M. Boughton, "The IMF and the Silent Revolution: Global Finance and Development in the 1980s" (Washington, DC: The International Monetary Fund), September 11, 2000, www.imf.org/external/pubs/ft/silent/index.htm.

18 Richard N. Swift, "United States Leadership in the United Nations", *The Western Political Quarterly*, Vol. 11, No. 2, 1958, pp. 183–194, https://doi.org/10.2307/444400.

19 As reported in Philip C. Jessup, "The Berlin Blockade and the Use of the United Nations", *Foreign Affairs*, October 1971, www.foreignaffairs.com/articles/europe/1971-10-01/berlin-blockade-and-use-united-nations.

20 Larry Blomstedt, "Into Korea", in Larry Blomstedt, *Truman, Congress, and Korea: The Politics of America's First Undeclared War* (Lexington, KY: University Press of Kentucky), 2016, pp. 23–54, https://doi.org/10.2307/j.ctt189ttn6.5; Richard C. Snyder and Glenn D. Paige, "The United States Decision to Resist Aggression in Korea: The Application of an Analytical Scheme", *Administrative Science Quarterly*, Vol. 3, December 1958, pp. 341–378.

21 Leland M. Goodrich, "The United Nations and the Korean War: A Case Study", *Proceedings of the Academy of Political Science*, Vol. 25, No. 2, 1953, pp. 90–104, www.jstor.org/stable/1173269.

22 "Address by President Dwight Eisenhower to the U.N. General Assembly", Address at the Tenth Anniversary Meeting of the United Nations, San Francisco, CA (Washington, DC: U.S. Department of State), June 20, 1955, https://2009-2017.state.gov/p/io/potusunga/207329.htm.

23 C.D. Jackson Papers, Box 30, "Atoms for Peace—Evolution (5)"; NAID #12021574, www.eisenhowerlibrary.gov/sites/default/files/research/online-documents/atoms-for-peace/atoms-for-peace-draft.pdf.

24 Richard N. Swift, "United States Leadership in the United Nations", p. 184.

25 Inis L. Claude, "The United Nations, the United States, and the Maintenance of Peace", *International Organization*, Vol. 23, No. 3, 1969, pp. 621–636, www.jstor.org/stable/2706073.

26 Ross N. Berkes, "The United Nations and the Cold War Conflict", *Current History*, Vol. 37, No. 218, 1959, pp. 228–238, www.jstor.org/stable/45310332.

27 M. S. Rajan and T. Israel, "The United Nations and the Conflict in Vietnam", in Richard A. Falk, Ed., *The Vietnam War and International Law, Volume 4: The Concluding Phase* (Princeton, NJ: Princeton University Press), 1976, pp. 114–144.

28 Henry Kissinger, *Diplomacy* (New York: Simon & Schuster), 1994, pp. 249–250; Marc Trachtenberg, "The Berlin Crisis", in Marc Trachtenberg, *History and Strategy* (Princeton, NJ: Princeton University Press), 1991, pp. 169–234.

29 Edward Keefer, "Foreign Relations of the United States (FRUS), 1969–76", *Foundations of Foreign Policy*, Vol. I, 1972, Doc 2, www.diplomatie.gouv.fr/IMG/pdf/ONU_edward_keefer.pdf.

30 Seyom Brown, *Faces of Power: United States Foreign Policy from Truman to Clinton* (New York: Columbia University Press), 1994, 2nd ed., pp. 298–302; Daniel J. Sargent, "North/South: The United States Responds to the New International Economic Order", *Humanity*, Spring 2015, Vol. 6, No. 1, pp. 201–216.

31 Quoted in Samuel S. Kim, *China, the United Nations and World Order* (Princeton, NJ: Princeton University Press), 1979, p. 104.

32 Henry Kissinger, *Diplomacy*, pp. 713–732.

33 Susan V. Lawrence and Caitlin Campbell, "Taiwan: Political and Security Issues" (Washington, DC: Congressional Research Service), June 13, 2023.

34 Richard Bush, "A One-China Policy Primer" (Washington, DC: The Brookings Institution), March 2017, www.brookings.edu/wp-content/uploads/2017/03/one-china-policy-primer-web-final.pdf.

35 Henry Kissinger, *Diplomacy*, pp. 704–714; 742–743.

36 Seyom Brown, *Faces of Power*, 1994.

37 "Address by President Jimmy Carter to the U.N. General Assembly" (Washington, DC: U.S. Department of State), March 17, 1977, https://2009-2017.state.gov/p/io/potusunga/207272.htm#:~:text =The%20search%20for%20peace%20and,is%20solely%20 its%20own%20business.

38 David F. Schmitz and Vanessa Walker, "Jimmy Carter and the Foreign Policy of Human Rights: The Development of a Post-Cold War Foreign Policy", *Diplomatic History*, Vol. 28, No. 1, January 2004, pp. 122, 126–127, 136, www.jstor.org/stable/24914773?read-now= 1&oauth_data=eyJlbWFpbCI6Im13c2lzc29uQGdtYWlsLmNvbSIsI mluc3RpdHV0aW9uIjpbXSwicHJvdmlkZXIiOiJnb29nbGUi fQ&seq=10#page_scan_tab_contents.

39 Ibid., pp. 126–127, 136.

40 Ibid., p. 127.

41 Brian Hilton, " 'Maximum Flexibility for Peaceful Change': Jimmy Carter, Taiwan, and the Recognition of the People's Republic of China", *Diplomatic History*, Vol. 33, No. 4, 2009, pp. 595–613, www.jstor.org/stable/44214071; Yael S. Aronoff, "In Like a Lamb, Out Like a Lion: The Political Conversion of Jimmy Carter", *Political Science Quarterly*, Vol. 121, No. 3, 2006, pp. 425–449, www. jstor.org/stable/20202726.

42 Schmitz and Walker, "Jimmy Carter and the Foreign Policy of Human Rights", p. 130; Hilton, "Maximum Flexibility for Peaceful Change", pp. 601, 605.

43 Yael S. Aronoff, "In Like a Lamb, Out like a Lion".

44 Daniel J. Sargent, *Superpower Transformed* (New York: Oxford University Press), 2015.

45 President Reagan once responded to a remark proposing that the United States would welcome the departure of U.N. headquarters from Manhattan by saying "if they chose to leave, goodbye". Francis X. Clines, "For U.N. at 40, Mixed Message from Reagan", *The New York Times*, September 17, 1985, www.nytimes.com/1985/09/17/ world/for-un-at-40-mixed-message-from-reagan.html.

46 Lou Cannon, "Reagan: 'Peace through Strength'", *The Washington Post*, August 19, 1980, www.washingtonpost.com/archive/ politics/1980/08/19/reagan-peace-through-strength/f343ddc5-fbda-49fc-a524-6fbc29dfb312/.

47 "Aid to Greece and Turkey".

48 As written in NSC68, the report presented to President Harry S. Truman in 1950, which set the direction of U.S. national security policy in the Cold War:

The absence of order among nations is becoming less and less tolerable. This fact imposes on us, in our own interests, the responsibility of world leadership. It demands that we make the attempt, and accept the risks inherent in it, to bring about order and justice by means consistent with the principles of freedom and democracy". "NSC 68: United States Objectives and Programs for National Security.

49 Charles Krauthammer, "The Reagan Doctrine", *The Washington Post*, July 19, 1985, www.washingtonpost.com/archive/politics/ 1985/07/19/the-reagan-doctrine/b2a06583-46fd-41e5-b70d-c949dd3c50c2/; Fareed Zakaria, "The Reagan Strategy of Containment", *Political Science Quarterly*, Vol. 105, No. 3, 1990, pp. 373–395.

50 NSC68, 1950; Barry R. Posen and Stephen Van Evera, "Defense Policy and the Reagan Administration: Departure from Containment", *International Security*, Vol. 8, No. 1, 1983, pp. 3–45, https://doi.org/10.2307/2538484.

51 Paul Lewis, "World Court Supports Nicaragua after U.S. Rejected Judge's Role", *The New York Times*, June 28, 1986, Section 1, Page 1.

52 James Rosen, "The Icon the Republicans Want to Forget", *The New York Times*, August 28, 2004, www.nytimes.com/2004/08/28/ opinion/the-icon-the-republicans-want-to-forget.html.

53 Lou Cannon, "Reagan's Peace with the U.N.", *The Washington Post*, September 26, 1988, www.washingtonpost.com/archive/politics/ 1988/09/26/reagans-peace-with-the-un/d2561843-6002-41b5-b810-2c3a0958b2a2/; Robert C. Johansen, "The Reagan Administration and the U.N.: The Costs of Unilateralism", *World Policy Journal*, Vol. 3, No. 4, 1986, pp. 601–641, www.jstor.org/stable/40209032.

54 Howard La Franchi, "Bush and the U.N.: A Reluctant Embrace", *The Christian Science Monitor*, September 22, 2008, www.csmonitor.com/USA/Politics/2008/0922/p03s02-uspo.html.

55 "National Security Decision Directive Number 75: U.S. Relations with the USSR" (Washington, DC: The White House), January 17, 1983.

56 Ariel Akerman, Joao Paulo Pessoa, and Leonardo Welle, "The West's Teeth: IMF Conditionality during the Cold War", *The World Economy*, Vol. 45, March 15, 2022, pp. 2034–2051, https://doi.org/10.1111/twec.13264.

57 Sarah Babb, "The Washington Consensus as Transnational Policy Paradigm: Its Origins, Trajectory and Likely Successor", *Review of International Political Economy*, Vol. 12, No. 2, April 2013, pp. 268–297, www.jstor.org/stable/pdf/42003294.pdf?casa_token=Mxq yyy0mS58AAAAA:KAve_Xtsi9OBD0T3H4ba0pTVX7K9TFXD M7E2ZzHjsCTYZq_zOsyg_eEDPjqVcTTbp2w3I6RAz_cdi_vb-5CWdvtL8gSduTMMnRDYNuqjlvmPD7n7hucJ.

58 Michael M. Harrison, "Reagan's World", *Foreign Policy*, No. 43, Summer 1981, pp. 3–16, www.jstor.org/stable/1148246; R. Pee and William Michael Schmidli, "Introduction: The Reagan Administration and Democracy Promotion", in R. Pee and William Michael

Schmidli, Eds., *The Reagan Administration, the Cold War, and the Transition to Democracy Promotion* (Cham: Palgrave Macmillan), 2019, pp. 1–28.

59 "Out of These Troubled Times . . . A New World Order", *The Washington Post*, September 11, 1990, www.washingtonpost.com/archive/politics/1990/09/12/bush-out-of-these-troubled-times-a-new-world-order/b93b5cf1-e389-4e6a-84b0-85f71bf4c946/.

60 Richard N. Haass, "What to Do with American Primacy" (Washington, DC: The Brookings Institution), September 1, 1999, www.brookings.edu/articles/what-to-do-with-american-primacy/.

61 Tony Smith, *America's Mission: The United States and the Worldwide Struggle for Democracy in the Twentieth Century* (Princeton, NJ: Princeton University Press), 1994, pp. 318–319.

62 President George H. W. Bush, "Remarks to the Reserve Officers Association, January 23, 1991", George H. W. Bush Presidential Library & Museum, Public Papers.

63 Eric A. Miller and Steve A. Yetiv, "The New World Order in Theory and Practice: The Bush Administration's Worldview in Transition", *Presidential Studies Quarterly*, Vol. 31, No. 1, 2001, pp. 56–68.

64 David Hoffman and Ann Devroy, "Bush Rejects New Sanctions for China, Clears Satellites", *The Washington Post*, December 20, 1989, pp. 119–133, www.washingtonpost.com/archive/politics/1989/12/20/bush-rejects-ne w-sanctions-for-china-clears-satellites/4fc38781-546c-4b28-8863-fc9417d69ad7/; Jim Anderson, "Capitol Hill Calls for Stronger Actions on China", *UPI*, June 22, 1989, www.upi.com/Archives/1989/06/22/Capitol-Hill-calls-for-stronger-actions-on-China/3446614491200/; James B. Steinberg, "What Went Wrong? U.S.-China Relations from Tiananmen to Trump", *Texas National Security Review*, Vol. 3, No. 1, 2019/2020, https://tnsr.org/2020/01/what-went-wrong-u-s-china-relations-from-tiananmen-to-trump/.

65 Strobe Talbott, "Democracy and the National Interest", *Foreign Affairs*, November 1, 1996, www.foreignaffairs.com/united-states/democracy-and-national-interest; Rasmus Sinding Sondergaard, "Bill Clinton's 'Democratic Enlargement' and the Securitisation of Democracy Promotion", *Diplomacy & Statecraft*, Vol. 26, No. 3, 2015, pp. 534–551, https://doi.org/10.1080/09592296.2015.106 7529; Annika E. Poppe, "Democracy Promotion from Clinton to Bush", in Annika E. Poppe, *Whither to, Obama? U.S. Democracy Promotion after the Cold War* (Frankfurt: The Peace Research Institute), 2010, pp. 10–17, www.jstor.org/stable/pdf/resrep14541.5.pdf; Tony Smith, *America's Mission: The United States and the Worldwide Struggle for Democracy in the Twentieth Century*, pp. 324–326.

66 William J. Clinton, "Address to the Nation on Haiti", *The American Presidency Project*, September 15, 1994, www.presidency.ucsb.edu/documents/address-the-nation-haiti.

67 "Transcript: Clinton Addresses Nation on Yugoslavia Strike", *CNN*, March 24, 1999, https://edition.cnn.com/ALLPOLITICS/stories/1999/03/25/clinton.transcript/.

68 Elain Sciolino, "U.S. Narrows Terms for its Peacekeepers", *The New York Times*, September 23, 1993, www.nytimes. com/1993/09/23/world/us-narrows-terms-for-its-peacekeepers.html.
69 Anna J. Schwartz, "Time to Terminate the ESF and the IMF" (Washington, DC: National Bureau of Economic Research), August 26, 1998, www.cato.org/sites/cato.org/files/pubs/pdf/fpb-048.pdf; Art Pine, "Top U.S. Officials Urge Congress to Boost IMF Funds", *Los Angeles Times*, January 31, 1998, www.latimes.com/archives/ la-xpm-1998-jan-31-fi-13892-story.html.
70 "President Bush's Second Inaugural Address", January 20, 2005; Condoleezza Rice, "The Promise of Democratic Peace", *The Washington Post*, December 11, 2005, www.washingtonpost. com/archive/opinions/2005/12/11/the-promise-of-democratic-peace/72b0648b-50a0-4c6f-9956-e3dd3f4d572c/.
71 "The National Security Strategy of the United States of America" (Washington, DC: The White House), September 2002, https://2009-2017.state.gov/documents/organization/63562.pdf; Strobe Talbott, "Unilateralism: Anatomy of a Foreign Policy Disaster" (Washington, DC: The Brookings Institution), February 21, 2007, www.brookings. edu/articles/unilateralism-anatomy-of-a-foreign-policy-disaster/.
72 During his eight years in office, President Bush oversaw the U.S. withdrawal from the Anti-Ballistic Missile treaty and the Kyoto Protocol on climate change, and declined to formally join the International Criminal Court (ICC).
73 "Institutionalizing the Freedom Agenda: President Bush Calls on Future Presidents and Congresses to Continue Leading the Cause of Freedom Worldwide" (Washington, DC: U.S. Department of State), July 17, 2008, https://2001-2009.state.gov/r/pa/prs/ps/2008/ oct/110871.htm.
74 The W. Bush administration's Millenium Challenge Account (MCA) was designed to increase the provision of U.S. development aid. Its terms include conditions meant to foster market-oriented changes as well as recipient government investments in the health and well-being of its citizens. Esther Pan, "Foreign Aid: Millennium Challenge Account Backgrounder" (New York: Council on Foreign Relations), February 7, 2005, www.cfr.org/backgrounder/ foreign-aid-millennium-challenge-account.
75 Barry Eichengreen and Douglas A. Irwin, "International Economic Policy: Was There a Bush Doctrine?" (Cambridge, MA: National Bureau of Economic Research), Working paper 13831, March 2008, Abstract, www.nber.org/papers/w13831.
76 Ibid., p. 31.
77 Stephen Schlesinger, "Bush's Stealth United Nations Policy", *World Policy Journal*, Vol. 25, No. 2, 2008, p. 8, www.jstor.org/stable/40210173. pdf?casa_token=FTqVFShjcfYAAAAA:Pxhh5jFERKvwRq3BBmlIw wmVpSMlFZ10aEzWG2RL8yX-bAVQviqf45gcm__dwfASzuR4Vr2t WzfiXLLaj4khqbZASV1FaKrgF_C4wqGjNaRKVhr9rAB; Howard La Franchi, "Bush and the U.N.: A Reluctant Embrace".

78 Douglas A. Rediker, "Why US Multilateral Leadership Was Key to the Global Financial Crisis Response" (Washington, DC: The Brookings Institution), September 12, 2018, www.brookings.edu/articles/why-us-multilateral-leadership-was-key-to-the-global-financial-crisis-response/.

79 Each of these themes figures prominently in Obama's last speech as president before the U.N. General Assembly. "Address by President Obama to the 71st Session of the United Nations General Assembly" (New York: The United Nations), September 20, 2016, https://obamawhitehouse.archives.gov/the-press-office/2016/09/20/address-president-obama-71st-session-united-nations-general-assembly.

80 Martin Indyk, Kenneth Lieberthal, and Michael E. O'Hanlon, "Scoring Obama's Foreign Policy", *Foreign Affairs*, April 20, 2012, www.foreignaffairs.com/united-states/scoring-obamas-foreign-policy?gclid=Cj0KCQiAo-yfBhD_ ARIsANr56g7hDncJ1bZTsBQY7y omAoADI52wQb-_ lLFHgYldmuuf7iJxE2GVNnkaAt-4EALw_wcB; Thomas Carothers, "Democracy Policy Under Obama: Revitalization or Retreat" (Washington, DC: Carnegie Endowment for International Peace), January 11, 2012, https://carnegieendowment.org/2012/01/11/democracy-policy-under-obama-revitalization-or-retreat-pub-46443; "Remarks by President Obama in Address to the United Nations General Assembly" (Washington, DC: The White House), September 24, 2014, https://obamawhitehouse.archives.gov/the-press-office/2014/09/24/remarks-president-obama-address-united-nations-general-asSembly; "Address by President Obama to the 71st Session of the United Nations General Assembly"; Scott W. Harold, "The Legacy Obama Leaves His Successor in Asia" (Washington, DC: RAND Corporation), October 26, 2016, www.rand.org/pubs/commentary/2016/10/the-legacy-obama-leaves-his-successor-in-asia.html.

81 This did result in the destruction of large quantities of chemical weapons, but not all of them, and neither did it prevent Assad from using them again in 2017 and 2018.

82 Sarah Begley, "Read Donald Trump's Speech to AIPAC", *Time*, March 21, 2016, https://time.com/4267058/donald-trump-aipac-speech-transcript/.

83 Ryan Hass and Abraham Denmark, "More Pain than Gain: How the US-China Trade War Hurt America" (Washington, DC: The Brookings Institution), August 7, 2020, www.brookings.edu/articles/more-pain-than-gain-how-the-us-china-trade-war-hurt-america/#:~:text=Economic%20costs%20of%20the%20trade,t%20hire%20as%20many%20people.

84 Tom McTague and Peter Nicholas, "How 'America First' Became America Alone", *The Atlantic*, October 29, 2020, www.theatlantic.com/international/archive/2020/10/donald-trump-foreign-policy-america-first/616872/; Eli Watkins, "Trump Taunts North Korea: My Nuclear Button Is 'Much Bigger', 'More Powerful'", *CNN*, January 3, 2018, www.cnn.com/2018/01/02/politics/donald-trump-north-korea-nuclear/index.html.

85 Peter Baker, "Favoring Foes over Friends, Trump Threatens to Upend International Order", *The New York Times*, February 11, 2024, www.nytimes.com/2024/02/11/us/politics/trump-nato.html.
86 Inis L. Claude, "The United Nations, the United States, and the Maintenance of Peace"; "President George H.W. Bush Speaks to Congress about a 'New World Order' Address", United States Congress, March 6, 1991, https://wwnorton.com/college/history/america7_brief/content/multimedia/ch36/research_01d.htm; John R. Bolton, "The Global Prosecutors", *Foreign Affairs*, January 1, 1999, www.foreignaffairs.com/reviews/review-essay/1999-01-01/global-prosecutors?check_logged_in=1; "Full Transcript: Donald Trump at the United Nations General Assembly", September 25, 2018, www.theatlantic.com/international/archive/2018/09/trump-unga-transcript-2018/571264/; Bruce Jones, "American Sovereignty Is Safe from the UN", *Foreign Affairs*, September 28, 2018, www.foreignaffairs.com/united-states/american-sovereignty-safe-un; Stephen Schlesinger, "Bush's Stealth United Nations Policy", pp. 1–9; "Remarks by DNSA Avril D. Haines at Yale Law School on the Importance of Treaties", Yale Law School, October 15, 2016, https://obamawhitehouse.archives.gov/the-press-office/2016/10/19/remarks-dnsa-avril-d-haines-yale-law-school-importance-treaties.
87 For a comprehensive accounting, see: "Arms Control and Nonproliferation: A Catalog of Treaties and Agreements", Congressional Research Service, April 25, 2022, https://sgp.fas.org/crs/nuke/RL33865.pdf; Mathew Evangelista, "Transnational Organizations and the Cold War", in Melvyn P. Leffler and Odd Arne Westad, Eds., *The Cold War: Volume III* (Cambridge: Cambridge University Press), 2010, Chapter 19, pp. 400–421.
88 David Skidmore, "The Obama Presidency and US Foreign Policy: Where's the Multilateralism?", *International Studies Perspectives*, Vol. 13, No. 1, 2012, pp. 43–64, www.jstor.org/stable/pdf/44218678.pdf?casa_token=6Y6EqD-iBQsAAAAA:-uA0OyD3jWXYb7d_MCFAE5xMRBXaE1T2Xar7OXHEJf4n06CeufKUEzi8ycAOVgzB5mlIgSSQIEsWxfzEUMqavdD8XDhghUPRTDY-1UPXoyyqU0rwjTED; Rosa Brooks, "Drones and the International Rule of Law", *Ethics and International Affairs*, Vol. 28, 2014, pp. 83–104, https://scholarship.law.georgetown.edu/cgi/viewcontent.cgi?article=2296&context=facpub; Carol Rosenberg, "Conditions at Guantanamo Are Cruel and Inhuman, U.N. Investigation Finds", *The New York Times*, June 26, 2023, www.nytimes.com/2023/06/26/us/politics/gitmo-prisoners-united-nations.html?smid=nytcore-ios-share&referringSource=articleShare; Joshua Rovner, "Has the United States Abandoned Arms Control?", *War on the Rocks*, June 2, 2020, https://warontherocks.com/2020/06/has-the-united-states-abandoned-arms-control/; Examples include but are not limited to the Rome Statute of the International Criminal Court, the U.N. Convention on the Law of the Sea, the Convention on Cluster Munitions, the Anti-Personnel Mine Ban Convention, the

Rights of the Child Convention, the Convention on the Rights of Persons with Disabilities; the World Health Organization; the Paris climate agreement; and the Trans-Pacific Partnership.

89 Anya Wahal, "On International Treaties, the United States Refuses to Play Ball" (New York: Council on Foreign Relations), January 7, 2022, www.cfr.org/blog/international-treaties-united-states-refuses-play-ball.

90 "Funding the United Nations: How Much Does the U.S. Pay?" (New York: Council on Foreign Relations), March 13, 2023, www.cfr.org/article/funding-united-nations-what-impact-do-us-contributions-have-un-agencies-and-programs.

91 David Vine, "Where in the World Is the U.S. Military?", *Politico*, July/August 2015, www.politico.com/magazine/story/2015/06/us-military-bases-around-the-world-119321/; Mohammed Hussein and Mohammed Haddad, "Infographic: U.S. Military Presence around the World", *Al Jazeera*, September 10, 2021, www.aljazeera.com/news/2021/9/10/infographic-us-military-presence-around-the-world-interactive.

92 Hans M. Kristensen and Matt Korda, "Nuclear Notebook: United States Nuclear Weapons, 2020", January 1, 2020, https://the-bulletin.org/premium/2020-01/nuclear-notebook-united-states-nuclear-forces-2020/.

93 Dispute settlement reports within the framework of GATT 1947, The World Trade Organization: www.wto.org/english/tratop_e/dispu_e/gt47ds_e.html.

94 Hunter, Jr, Richard J., Hector R. Lozada, and John H. Shannon, "The Debate on Reforms of the WTO Appellate Process: A Proxy for a More Serious Discussion of the Future of the WTO", *Economics and Business Quarterly Reviews*, Vol. 6, No. 1, 2023, February 10, 2023, pp. 86–105, available at SSRN, https://ssrn.com/abstract=4353775.

95 Jean-Marc Thouvenin, "History of Implementation of Sanctions", and Richard Nephew, "Implementation of Sanctions: United States", in Masahiko Asada, Ed., *Economic Sanctions in International Law and Practice* (New York: Routledge), 2020, pp. 83–115, https://library.oapen.org/viewer/web/viewer.html?file=/bitstream/handle/20.500.12657/52777/9780429629655.pdf?sequence=1&isAllowed=y.

96 T. Clifton Morgan, Navin Bapat, and Yoshi Kobayashi, "The Threat and Imposition of Sanctions: Updating the TIES Dataset", *Conflict Management and Peace Science*, Vol. 31, No. 5, 2014, pp. 541–558.

97 "Remarks by National Security Advisor Jake Sullivan on the Biden-Harris Administration's National Security Strategy" (Washington, DC: The White House), October 12, 2022, www.whitehouse.gov/briefing-room/speeches-remarks/2022/10/13/remarks-by-national-security-advisor-jake-sullivan-on-the-biden-harris-administrations-national-security-strategy/; "Remarks by National Security Advisor Jake Sullivan on Renewing American Economic Leadership at the Brookings

Institution" (Washington, DC: The Brookings Institution), April 27, 2023, www.whitehouse.gov/briefing-room/speeches-remarks/2023/04/27/remarks-by-national-security-advisor-jake-sullivan-on-renewing-american-economic-leadership-at-the-brookings-institution/; "Speech by Antony J. Blinken, Secretary of State: The Administration's Approach to the People's Republic of China" (Washington, DC: The U.S. Department of State), May 26, 2022, www.state.gov/the-administrations-approach-to-the-peoples-republic-of-china/; "Remarks by President Biden on the United Efforts of the Free World to Support the People of Ukraine" (Washington, DC: The White House), March 26, 2022, www.whitehouse.gov/briefing-room/speeches-remarks/2022/03/26/remarks-by-president-biden-on-the-united-efforts-of-the-free-world-to-support-the-people-of-ukraine/#:~:text=It%20was%20a%20long%2C%20painful,need%20to%20be%20clear%2Deyed.

4

CHINA

* * *

China, as the country is defined on a map today, is very big and very populous. China, as a civilization, not only is very big and very populous but is also very, very old. Chinese civilization dates roughly to the year 2000 BCE, a continuity of history that exceeds that of the United States by almost 4,000 years.[1] The two modern nations' philosophical origins, however, date much more closely together. It was around the time that Plato was germinating Western political thought in ancient Greece that Confucius was doing the same in China.[2] Much as Plato was the well-spring of what followed in the West, so too did the work of Confucius initiate centuries of contemplation in Asia about the mysteries of human nature, the problems of ordering social life, and the relationship between the two.

The philosophies that developed in ancient China were just as concerned with reconciling political order with human well-being and happiness as were the philosophies that developed in the ancient West.[3] Those working in China, especially when living through troubled times marked by social instability and violence, were focused on elaborating the Dao—on providing a guide for the "right" way for humans to live, and to live together.[4] Their explorations in metaphysics, mindfulness, virtue, and law have influenced Chinese life ever since. Although China's short modern history is sharply different to that of its long past, ancient traditions of thought remain visible in Chinese society and politics in the present day. Themes of self-discipline and self-abnegation, prioritization of community well-being, prizing of unity, intolerance of chaos, comfort with hierarchy, and attachment to ritual are all recognizable in modern China.[5]

The Chinese people have a very long history with a form of politics in which authority is highly centralized and in which individuals are

DOI: 10.4324/9781032723358-4

subject to considerable behavioral limitations and demands. To dismiss this form of social order as objectionable without first examining the problems it is believed to solve and the principles and values upon which it is built is to be willfully blind to the fact that those principles and values have proved compelling for billions of people who, over thousands of years, have believed in them, have taken pride in them, and have fought and died for them. These principles, moreover, combine with China's lived history to shape its engagement with the world. In the modern era, they are evident in its pursuit of an international order that, its leaders believe, will provide Chinese citizens with socioeconomic stability and insulate the state against the intrusions of disruptive external agents and influences.

Harmony, Hierarchy, and Law

Confucius is the ancient philosopher most associated with China today, but however unique and remarkable the durability and extent of his influence, he was not singular in shaping many of the core concepts and convictions that animate Chinese political thought. He, his direct disciples, and his critics lived and wrote during a fractious 550 years, a period during which the Chinese empire had devolved into smaller units whose leaders vied for wealth and power by all means available—theft, trickery, alliance, and violence. Various accounts place the number of wars that occurred during those centuries at somewhere between 400 and 1700.[6]

According to the commonly held metaphysical understanding of the origins of authority at the time, this collapse of human civilization stood in contravention to the mandate of Heaven.[7] For Confucius, the fact that heaven was infallible led inexorably to the conclusion that disorder was the product of human indolence, error, and pursuit of self-interest. Harmony with heaven, therefore, could only be restored through the self-cultivation of virtue, which required each individual to recognize and to behave in accordance not with his own drives and desires but rather with the universe's hierarchy in relation to heaven and in relation to one another. It was hierarchy's behavioral demands, in other words, and each individual's discipline in the practice of them, that would provide structure and purpose to social interactions and thereby render them peaceable.[8]

Social order thus depended upon each person's devotion to perfecting his knowledge of his role in the universe and in his community, and upon his commitment to properly engaging in the rites and rituals of those roles. The rulers in whom authority was entrusted by heaven, too and especially, were subject to the demands of virtue. It was the visibility of their violations that would degrade order, and their demonstrations of achievement that would extend its depth, breadth, and duration.[9]

The power of moral example was not, for Confucius, fantasy or idealism. It was a return to the ordering principle that had served Chinese civilization well over the thousands of years of its history; social order created by the benevolence and virtue of leaders was eminently achievable because it had already been achieved.[10]

Not all thinkers were as convinced as Confucius about the ordering effects of moral righteousness. For many, and in particular for a group labeled Legalists, the conclusion to be drawn from the period's relentless brutality was that while it may be better to have a moral leader than an immoral one, in either case it is unity of authority that is necessary for order. Legalism's proposition is that the possession and use of wealth and power by one ruler is the only means through which to manage the otherwise ruinous effects of individual pursuit of self-interest. It is therefore incumbent upon a powerful leader to establish norms of behavior and to distribute punishments and rewards accordingly. So long as the leader is consistent in the application of retribution for deviations from those norms and in the distribution of praise, prosperity, and promotion for obeisance to them, then the people will have no basis for complaint and social order will obtain.[11]

The Confucian and Legalist paradigms have divergent views about many elements of social life and are in wild disagreement with each other about the ability of humans to be self-regulating. Their positions on this question have very different implications for the structuring of political order.[12] Nonetheless, the traditions share three core convictions: that hierarchy culminating in unity of authority is necessary; that merit—whether measured by moral purity or by obedience to command—should determine hierarchy; and that a ruler's legitimacy derives from his competence in generating order and prosperity for the people and inspiring cultural achievement. If a ruler fails to perform, moreover—if the well-being and happiness of the people suffer—the people are justified in attempting to depose him. If the rebellion fails, then the ruler is proved to retain the mandate of heaven and can do as he sees fit to the rebels. If the rebellion succeeds, however, then the mandate is lost. In such instances, the chaos of revolution, the ugly business of regime replacement, and the national weakness inherent in such transitions are the necessary, if undesirable, outcomes of poor leadership.[13]

Confucianism and Legalism were variously in and out of favor over time and, in fact, were used together pragmatically during the period of state consolidation under the Han Dynasty, which lasted 400 years, including the first 200 of the common era (CE).[14] The Han dynasty was itself variously in and out of power thereafter, and China's experience in its absence produced an association of disunity with chaos and vulnerability to foreign invasion.[15]

For the duration, China was developing an economy that by the time of real connection with Europe in the 1500s was extremely well established, built on thriving, populous cities with productive infrastructure, large markets, and trade routes on land and sea that connected China to Southeast Asia, India, and the Middle East.[16] This was the industrious and wealthy China the Portuguese encountered upon their arrival along China's southern coast in 1517. Over the next century, much of the rest of Europe would follow, also in search of trade—first the Spanish, then the Dutch, British, and French. There were of course some disagreements and rough adjudications thereof along the way, but trade relations progressed largely unimpeded for three centuries.

So too did China's understanding of world order. Far from being moved by exposures to European missionaries, European traders, and even, in the late 1700s, European statesmen, their 2,000-year-old understanding of the mandate of heaven and China's position at the top of the universal hierarchy remained fixed. In the face of British pressure to adapt to Western modes of ordered interstate relations at the end of the century, China's emperor proved willing and wary.[17] He instructed his court to tolerate many of Britain's demands and to overlook many instances of its emissary's missteps—and occasional intransigence— concerning Chinese culture and custom. The emperor paired this magnanimity, however, with a missive sent directly to King George reminding him that China had no real need to trade with Britain. China, the King would do well to recall, could be very content with its own wealth and could happily confine its trade to those more malleable of the European nations. If Britain wanted continued access to China's markets, then Britain would have to be more mindful of doing so on China's terms.

This relationship changed dramatically in the early 1800s when Great Britain achieved such success in introducing its opium products into China that it disrupted civil society and longstanding patterns of Chinese international trade.[18] China's efforts to remedy the problem proved highly ineffective at resolving the damaging effects of opium imports but highly effective at provoking a militarized British response. The Opium Wars that followed (1839–1842 and 1856–1860), together with the organic weakening of the Qing dynasty in the face of growing poverty and rebellion, produced Chinese acquiescence to the Western powers' degrading demands. This was the origin of the 150-year-long British colonization of Hong Kong and of the "unequal treaties" that favored the trade desires of Western nations over China's identity and interests.[19] These losses were followed by yet another at the end of the century, this time to Japan, with terms of defeat for China that included recognizing the independence of Korea, relinquishing the island of Taiwan, and entering into another round of unequal trade arrangements. China's long-held metaphysical belief in heavenly decree and in its status at the top of a universal hierarchy were no longer reconcilable with events.[20]

In addition to the immediate sociopolitical problems this change produced, it also had a profound effect on the development of Chinese nationalism. Received at the time as deep humiliations, the association of Chinese weakness with the loss of territory at the hands of Western imperialism would endure. It lasted through a period of latency as China worked to regain internal order and despite Mao's purposeful reinterpretation of history as one of the struggle between communism and capitalism. Depiction of China as having been preyed upon and as having been victim to Western aggression reemerged in the late 20th century and continued to regain prominence as the "century of humiliation" in taught narratives thereafter.[21]

China's Relationship with the Post–War Order, 1945–2020

Imperial China, then ruled by the Qing Dynasty, entered the 20th century faced with serious problems, some of its own making and others outside its control. Internally, it had been weakened by "traditional forces of dynastic decline, such as a succession of weak emperors, widespread corruption, frequent floods, and local rebellions".[22] Externally, the West's modern military and its economic interest in China combined over time to render the relationship not just extractive but also threatening. The 1894–1895 Sino-Japanese war, moreover, made distressingly clear that China's small, island neighbor had surpassed it in the adoption and application of new Western technologies. The Qing dynasty's subsequent attempts at governance reform, undertaken in the hope of modernizing China, served only to hasten revolution.[23]

The subsequent decade was marked by fitful attempts at reforming the conceptual basis and practical exercise of political authority in China and by popular rejections of both. In 1911, this dynamic proved unsustainable, and the empire disintegrated, replaced by the Republic of China (ROC) under the leadership of Sun Yat-sen, a man selected not by heaven but by the vagaries of revolutionary politics. This did not usher in a period of stability, as Sun's leadership quickly gave way to that of another who also was unable to maintain order. Central authority dissolved, and China spent the next three decades immersed in a violent struggle between the Soviet-backed Chinese Communist Party (CCP) and its opponents, the Kuomintang (KMT) nationalists.

In the midst of this upheaval, China was a peripheral participant but not a direct combatant in World War I.[24] Not so for World War II. In the late 1930s, Japan annexed Manchuria and invaded northern China. The Japanese bombing of Pearl Harbor in 1941 thus gave the United States common cause with China for the remainder of the war. Estimates of Chinese loss of life between 1937 and 1945 reach as high as 30 million people, with some killed in battle and others dying from hardship, deprivation, and disease.[25] The Kuomintang (KMT) was in ascendance during the war, and its leader, nationalist Chiang Kai-Shek, was actively engaged in the form of interstate politics that had been established by and was necessary to partner with the West during the conflict and to participate in international politics after it: state-centric, procedural, and representative. It was the KMT that represented the Republic of China (ROC) during the founding of the United Nations and that created and then held its seat on the five-member security council.[26]

The Cold War

In the aftermath of the war, in 1949, the long and destructive fight between Chinese communists and the KMT culminated in the latter's flight to Taiwan. The Taiwan Strait, 100 miles of water between the mainland's coast and the island, provided enough separation to stop the war but not enough to settle the political dispute. The PRC and the ROC each continued to maintain that it, alone, was the sole legitimate government of China and to reject the claim of the other. Neither, however, had the capability to cross the Strait and continue the war, and so it settled into a stalemate. The non-resolution of Taiwan's status added the island to an extant set of unresolved PRC maritime and territorial disputes—about Tibet, and along its borders with India, Vietnam, and the Soviet Union—that are claimed for the usual sort of geopolitical reasons but that also are endowed with the content of China's unique historical memory of the century of humiliation. These rational and emotional attachments shape the PRC's understanding of sovereignty and are reflected in its stringency about the demarcation of borders and its stridency about non-interference in internal affairs.[27]

With the ROC's flight to Taiwan, the newly entrenched communist government of the PRC under Mao Zedong faced an even more Westernized world order. The United States was remodeling Japan, planting its military around the globe, and leading the post-war institutions.

The emphasis on free trade presented an obvious problem for the Communist Party, and Mao was not interested in multilateral participation under terms that did not further the PRC's claim to Chinese sovereignty. He was, however, willing to engage in politicking in order to press the case and agitated actively to represent China at the U.N. by making direct appeals to the institution and trying to enlist the assistance of others.[28] The strategy shifted from activism to patience after the Korean War, with the hope that time would allow events outside, and, for the composition of the institution inside, to make its possession of the representative seat of China more possible and its participation thereafter much more fruitful. This remained the strategy through the early 1960s, during which time the PRC consistently declared its support for the principles of the U.N. Charter and equally consistently objected that the operations of the institution were dominated by the imperialist United States. This, it argued, often led the U.N. to behave contrary to its Charter and contrary to the pursuit of peace.[29]

As hoped, growth in the number of states within the General Assembly with which China's arguments had purchase coincided with a change in its external environment. In the early 1970s, the U.S. position on China was changing under the administration of Richard Nixon. When, in 1971, the United States signaled it would not object, the U.N. officially shifted recognition from the ROC on Taiwan to the PRC on the mainland.[30] Mao sent delegates to the U.N. in short order, and they and their successors spent much of the decade that followed observing and learning, using the institution as a forum to make its position on a select set of political issues known, but not to advocate for their realization.[31]

While Mao's strategy for advancing the PRC's global stature by gaining representation in the U.N. worked, his strategy for advancing the PRC's global stature by applying communist principles to the task of modernization failed terribly. In the cities he nationalized industry, in the countryside he collectivized agriculture, and in both places he ensured cooperation by establishing ruthless structures for enforcing ideological purity. The results of these attempts first, to industrialize through the Great Leap Forward (1958–1962), and then to strip the PRC of any vestiges of traditionalism through the Cultural Revolution (1966–1976), were disastrous. Tens of millions of people suffered the tortures of dying from starvation; communities were riven by fear, suspicion, and self-preservation; people were executed and committed suicide in large numbers; and China remained poor, agrarian, and absent the international respect and standing that Mao sought.[32] After Mao's death in 1976, with a country devastated by famine and ravaged by internal purges, the CCP pursued a different and less personalistic strategy for national development. This was true for their management of domestic and international affairs and was evident in their approach to the post war institutions.

At home, although Mao's successors retained Marxism-Leninism's emphasis on centralized authority and collectivism, they tried to reinforce both by catalyzing the productive energies of individual materialism and drive—to implement "socialism with Chinese characteristics".[33] This tacit embrace of the human desires for commodious living and personal accomplishment—in Chinese society measured by the extent of contribution to "the welfare and happiness of the people and to national prosperity", and not by individual fulfillment—was underwritten by an equally tacit embrace of the standards and practices of capitalist international economic relations.[34]

The 1979 normalization of relations with the United States, which made space for bilateral economic and diplomatic exchange, encouraged and facilitated this economic transition. In 1980, the PRC joined the World Bank and the IMF. Over the next two decades, China's economy grew dramatically. It became a trading nation; it attracted investment into its economy and invested large sums in the economies of others. It achieved this growth by adopting many of the tools and techniques of economic modernization that had been used effectively by Europe, the United States, and, increasingly, regional neighbors—Japan, Korea, Taiwan, Hong Kong, and Singapore.[35]

This transition toward market principles, however, was not undertaken wholesale. To the contrary, many economists have characterized China's development strategy as one that combined a new openness to imports with a longer history of closure to them, as it retained features of import-substituting industrialization (ISI)—the use of policy tools to insulate domestic industries against foreign competitors. It therefore maintained tariffs in critical sectors, tightly regulated imports, and kept strategic industries like telecommunications closed to foreign investment.[36]

Given the upward trajectory China's strategy had produced, it would have been imaginable if not understandable for it simply to continue operating its economy this way—connected with but still aloof from the industrialized global economy. Instead, beginning in 1986, China embarked upon an insistent and persistent campaign for accession into the General Agreement on Tariffs and Trade (GATT).[37] There are many possible explanations for this decision—an appetite for further accelerating economic growth, for example, a desire to improve domestic industry through the crucible of open market competition, attentiveness to the rising tide of expectations among Chinese citizens, pursuit of international status, and more—and they are not mutually exclusive.[38] Whatever the mixture of reasons, however, achieving the goal of accession, which China did in 2001, was costly. It meant, first, that China had to relax its insistence that the principle of sovereign non-interference required the operation of its domestic economy to remain apart from the operation of the global economy and instead to integrate by accepting multilateral rules and standards. It also required China to complete a program of demanding internal adjustments, removing tariff protections that had for decades defended its industries against international competition.[39]

It was during that same period that the nature of China's participation in, and its narrative about, the U.N. also began to change. By then China, having spent the early period studying and learning the ways of U.N. diplomacy, was more prepared and more inclined to practice it effectively. In the 1980s China began to accept multilateral aid, taking infusions of funds from the World Bank and various U.N. organs, and participated in U.N. conferences on functional issues—disarmament for example, and the Law of the Sea.[40] So too did Chinese leaders and diplomats begin to emphasize the relationship between peace, economic development, and multilateralism and to make overt official statements of support for the purposes and principles of the U.N. Charter.[41]

After the Cold War

China's initial movements into the post-war institutions were conditioned by the U.S.-Soviet Cold War, and thereafter by what the United States prefers to call its post–Cold War primacy but the PRC refers to as a period of U.S. hegemony. The transition from the one epoch to the other contained U.S. support for a democratic transition in Taiwan, the broadly aggressive democratization agenda of the Ronald Reagan administration, and the 1989 pro-democracy protests in Beijing's Tiananmen Square. Taken independently each would have profoundly influenced Beijing's perceptions of its international environment; coming in rapid succession they were not just influential but frightening and formative.

This was especially true of the protest movement, which China's most senior leaders not only perceived as socially destabilizing, and therefore as a personally and nationally existential threat, but also believed was the product of collusion between internal and external enemies. Those enemies very much included the United States, which, they were convinced, had the goal of destroying the CCP. The events in Tiananmen Square were evidence of "a well-planned plot whose real aim is to reject the Chinese Communist Party and the socialist system at the most fundamental level".[42] The U.S. imposition of sanctions and other measures after the CCP used force to clear protestors from the square, killing hundreds and possibly more, certainly did not diminish this perception, even though many in the United States argued that the U.S. response was mild and insufficiently punitive.[43]

The idea that the United States sought the internal liberalization of China and in general harbored ill-intent toward the CCP persisted through the collapse of the Soviet Union in 1991. This, together with America's post-Tiananmen insistence on advancing human rights and candidate Bill Clinton's emphasis on domestic economic discontent, precipitated in part by growing access to the Chinese market, predetermined that U.S.-China relations would be uneasy during the first term of the first fully post–Cold War president. Those expectations were not disappointed.[44] Recriminations were forthcoming from both sides on such issues as human rights, trade, and the status of Taiwan. In 1996 the latter moved from a verbal to a militarized exchange. The PRC launched missiles over the Taiwan Strait, and the United States responded by dispatching a carrier group to international waters nearby. That was the extent of it, but for both parties, it constituted enough of an upset to revisit their respective approaches to the Taiwan question.[45]

Throughout the 1990s, the PRC sought to moderate U.S. unilateralism by intensifying its own efforts to bolster multilateralism, first and foremost within the post-war institutions but also by proliferating its involvement in others. By 2000, China was a member of more than 1,300 multilateral organizations.[46] Within the U.N., China accepted new roles and responsibilities, acceded to treaties, and increased the presence and profile of its diplomats and leaders through attendance and speech-giving at key sessions.[47] When financial crisis struck East Asia in 1997, China responded by coordinating its efforts to offer loans with the IMF and refrained from devaluing its currency. This couldn't solve the problem, but it also didn't make it worse, and it reduced pressure on others to engage in a destructive race-to-the-bottom of currency depreciation.[48]

The second Clinton term was characterized by bilateral interest in stabilization, but this neither ameliorated concern within the PRC about U.S. power and the exercise of unilateralism it tempted, nor did it prevent the occasional flashpoint from arising. These converged in the form of the accidental bombing of the Chinese embassy in Belgrade during NATO's Kosovo campaign in 1999. The conflict itself was widely interpreted in China as yet more evidence that the United States was aggressively hegemonic. The bomb, which killed three Chinese staff, was quickly internalized as "a deliberate, calculated attack to punish China's opposition to the war, to destabilize and humiliate China, and to probe Beijing's external reaction and domestic response to the outburst of nationalism that the bombing was bound to ignite".[49]

The terrorist attacks on the United States of September 2001 changed the trajectory of geopolitics in ways that created opportunities and complications for China. Beijing responded in the immediate aftermath with expressions of sympathy, directly from President Jiang Zemin. It also supported U.N. Security Council resolutions condemning terrorism, condoning the U.S. military effort to remove the Taliban regime that had harbored the perpetrators in Afghanistan, and backing U.S. insistence that Iraqi president Saddam Hussein submit to inspections to confirm or deny the existence of weapons of mass destruction.[50] These positions went a non-trivial distance toward moderating what had been a steady decline in U.S.-China relations in the year preceding. But the period also quickly became dominated by the George W. Bush administration's ideological and activist foreign policy, which included two major localized wars, one in Afghanistan, one in Iraq, and another diffuse war against terrorist organizations worldwide. So too did the first decade of the 2000s include the 2008–2009 global financial crisis precipitated by a collapse in the decentralized and risk-acceptant U.S. financial system.[51]

China interpreted this collection of international activities and events, along with innumerable other policies of lesser immediate consequence but of a cumulative weight, as evidence of a U.S. strategy to perpetuate hegemony and the international order—defined by the risks of economic liberalization, the intrusiveness of democratic values, and the threat of forward-postured U.S. armed forces—that went with it. Militarily the United States retained its expansive Cold War footprint in Asia, entered into basing and deployment agreements with Singapore and Australia, and, in the 2010s, was openly stating its intent to further expand and enhance its regional reach.[52] U.S. involvement in disputes over competing maritime and territorial claims was increasing in frequency and becoming increasingly unwelcome, most especially in regard to the ongoing disagreement between the CCP and the government of Taiwan about Taiwan's international political status. Economically and diplomatically, the United States similarly was deepening its role in regional affairs, pursuing trade agreements and in other ways moving "boldly to shift the center of gravity among the key multilateral organizations in Asia, favoring those that include the United States and leading them to take approaches favored by Washington".[53] The CCP's conclusion was that the United States had determined that if not converting, then at least subduing and constraining the PRC was necessary for the United States to fulfill its hegemonic ambitions.[54]

The CCP found this American strategy objectionable and, especially in the years after Xi Jinping's 2012 ascension to the presidency, took measures to counter the success of what it saw as U.S. efforts to hinder China's internal development and to limit its external freedom of action.[55] Expressed as "Xi Jinping Thought", the approach was to improve the Party's unity and discipline so that it could effectively implement policies that would insulate China from an increasingly hostile international environment, resolve contradictions in China's economy—insufficient domestic demand, growing wealth inequality, and environmental degradation—and enhance the PRC's standing internationally.[56]

Development Abroad, and at Home

Economically, these goals were most visibly manifest in one big venture abroad and one at home. In 2013, China launched One Belt One Road (OBOR), now commonly referred to as the Belt and Road Initiative (BRI). Its purpose was to partner with countries in Central and West Asia, Europe, and Africa on infrastructure projects that would satisfy local needs and create economic benefit for China by engaging Chinese production capacity, creating export markets, and providing access to commodities and diversifying supply lines.[57] Because BRI is a vehicle for Chinese economic growth, it is considered by many to be more a feature of China's outward-oriented globalization than of its development aid agenda.[58]

Shortly thereafter, in 2015, the CCP initiated Made in China 2025, a ten-year plan for government subsidies and other incentives meant to catalyze growth in indigenous high technology manufacturing and innovation, most prominently in information and communications technologies and electric vehicles. Of a piece with its long history with ISI, the intent of Made in China was to reduce its dependence on external markets for the inputs it would need to generate economic growth and industrial competitiveness into the future.[59] While BRI has been criticized as being exploitative and extractive, Made in China 2025 has been criticized as protectionist—even if not necessarily in violation of the WTO—and dangerous.[60] While all WTO members engage in some degree of subsidization, there were two special concerns about Made in China 2025. The first was that some of its interventions were in industries with military applications. The second was that Made in China 2025 might make others, including and perhaps especially the United States, vulnerable to Chinese control over important, and limited supply chains.[61]

Boats, Bases, and Bombs

China also sought the objective of reinstating its status as a great power through the expansion and enhancement of its national military capabilities and through unyielding assertion of territorial claims. Modernization of the PLA began in earnest in the 1990s. The catalyst for the fact and the direction of these efforts was its internalization of lessons taken from the precision and mobility capabilities the United States used to great effect in the 1991 Gulf War. Over the subsequent three decades, this display—reinforced by demonstrations of U.S. military capability in the allied air campaign over Yugoslavia in 1999, its opening campaign in Afghanistan, and the return to Iraq in 2003—activated China's long-standing anxiety about defending the homeland. Recurrent tensions with the United States over the status of and activities within and around Taiwan exacerbated these fears.

Altogether, the effect was to convince China that the demands of prosecuting a local war with the United States would require a fundamental reconfiguration of the PLA from being mass-based in strategy, doctrine, and force structure to being organized, trained, and equipped to conduct "systems confrontation".[62] Its military budget thus grew from less than an estimated $20 billion in 1991 to more than an estimated $120 billion in 2011, and then to almost $250 billion by 2021.[63] The CCP also emphasized culling corrupt officials from leadership ranks, and adapting the PLA's force readiness, doctrine, and organizational structure to take advantage of modern information technologies. These capabilities were unified under the control of the PLA Strategic Support Force (SSF) in 2015, which was believed to be responsible for the PLA's satellite launch and operations, for network operations including electronic and cyber warfare and for the coordination and integration of the two.[64]

In 2012, the PRC also began to advance and expand its maritime power, seeking to build a naval fleet capable of safeguarding its maritime rights and interests. Those rights and interests were primarily, but not exclusively, localized in its near seas. In 2008, two Chinese commercial vessels were attacked by pirates around the Horn of Africa, and in 2011, the war in Libya cost China roughly $20 billion in infrastructure and telecommunications investments.[65] It was therefore attuned to defending against security risks when implementing BRI. Although military assistance had been part of its development programs in Africa since 2000, in 2017, China established its first overseas military base in Djibouti.[66] The PRC explained the base as intended to increase its ability to protect its assets, Chinese citizens living and working abroad, and to support its ongoing anti-piracy operations.[67]

More locally, it was during this same period that the PRC began transforming coral reefs in the South China Sea into artificial islands substantial enough to hold buildings, runways, and other infrastructure, both civilian and military. This campaign strengthened China's position relative to other regional claimants to disputed waters. It also created accessible landmasses that could be used by the PLA to defend, or deny, sea lines of communication to potential adversaries and to create strategic depth to aid in defense of the mainland.[68] After 2016, reports of tense incidents around these artificial islands and other maritime features became more common. These occurred between regional actors, the PLA, and its associated but technically unaffiliated maritime militia—a fleet of fishing and other non-naval ships that China has long used for coastal missions and sovereignty enforcement.[69]

So too did the PRC continue to use demonstrations of military capability in furtherance of its goal of unification with Taiwan. It engaged in persistent information operations intended to influence the population's perceptions of the Taiwan government, of mainland China, and of the United States. It intensified its efforts to curtail Taiwan's international relationships, using the threat of rescinding trade ties to deter other states from engaging with Taipei. It demonstrated that these threats were not idle when in 2021, after Lithuania established a Taiwan representative office in its capital Vilnius, Lithuanian exports to China decreased by a full 91%.[70] These measures were coupled with more regular and more sizable displays of military power around the island. There were new incursions into air and sea space controlled by the Taiwan government, often timed to demonstrate Beijing's objection to policies emanating from Taipei and from Washington D.C.

China has been a nuclear state since 1964, and it has since that time declared that it "will never at any time or under any circumstances be the first to use nuclear weapons".[71] Its nuclear posture was designed, from inception, to deter others from using or threatening to use nuclear weapons against it, and so it developed and maintained a notably small arsenal—roughly 200 to 300 warheads and delivery systems, as compared to the roughly 3,800 ready warheads and 800 delivery systems retained by the United States.[72] As explained in 1970 by Chinese premier Zhou Enlai:

> We are doing this to break the nuclear monopoly and nuclear blackmail, as well as to restrict the two superpowers. If we succeed, we will be able to suppress nuclear war and hopefully, ultimately eliminate nuclear weapons. . . . We are not using this to scare people, so we do not intend to produce large quantities, but we must still have a certain quantity, quality, and variety.[73]

In 2019, it became apparent that China was rapidly modernizing and expanding this arsenal. It began adding missile silos, growing its stockpile of warheads, and increasing its readiness to launch on short notice. These changes happened at a pace that the U.S. Department of Defense estimated would bring China's total stockpile to 1,000 nuclear weapons by 2030.[74] There is no consensus among experts about the reasons for this change in China's nuclear strategy, in part because the behavior is consistent with multiple explanations. It might indicate a desire to build an arsenal that will allow Beijing to use nuclear weapons coercively, by threatening a first strike.[75] Or, it might indicate insecurity about its ability to retaliate in the event of attack:

> China's own nuclear strategists and experts provide a different view of Chinese thinking. Their writings and analysis since 2015 suggest that China's nuclear expansion is less a shift in Chinese intentions than a response to what Beijing perceives as threatening changes in U.S. nuclear strategy . . . Chinese analysts are worried that the United States has lowered its threshold for nuclear use—including allowing for limited first use in a Taiwan conflict -and that the U.S. military is acquiring new capabilities that could be used to destroy or significantly degrade China's nuclear forces. Thus, many Chinese experts have concluded that China needs a more robust arsenal.[76]

Taken together, between 2012 and 2020, the PRC's international economic and security policies are consistent with a state responding to an environment in which it recognizes threats to its interests at the same time that it sees opportunities to advance them. China's policies, in other words, reflected its long-standing fears that the United States sought to bolster its own influence in Asia—bringing with it "liberal economics, liberal values and a U.S.-backed security community"—and its newfound confidence in resisting those efforts.[77] The result was a series of policies that were at turns defensive and activist, focused not just on securing China's material interests and sovereignty claims but also on advancing them.

China's Record of Compliance and Defiance

The PRC had a very different point of entry into the post–war order than did the United States. It was not present at the founding of the post-war institutions and was therefore neither a participant in forming their rules nor a party to the rules they formed. It was, instead, the Republic of China (ROC) on Taiwan, under the leadership of Kuomintang (KMT)

nationalists, that participated in deliberations about the post-war economic institutions before and at the Bretton Woods conference and that
created and then held China's seat on the five-member U.N. Security
Council from its founding until 1971.[78] Also unlike the United States,
when it did assume its seat on the Security Council, the PRC did so in a
position not of strength but one of weakness—in absolute and relative
terms.

The PRC of the early 1970s was underdeveloped, impoverished, and
still embroiled in the economically and socially destructive, personalist
rule of Mao Zedong. After Mao's death in 1976 and under the new
leadership of Deng Xiaoping, however, the PRC began what would
be a decades-long transformation of its domestic economy and of the
way in which it engaged with the outside world. To correct China's
"backwardness", Deng implemented substantial domestic reforms—
deconstructing communal agriculture, for example, and making space
for private entrepreneurialism—and began the process of integrating the
PRC into global economic and political society as an active member of
the post-war institutions.[79]

During and after this "opening and reform" period, China entered
into treaties, joined international organizations, and adapted its internal legal system to accommodate their rules—those that enabled it to
participate in institutional arrangements that support China's economic
growth or other interests without, of course, compromising its rigid
view of sovereign control over domestic affairs.[80] As the number of
China's institutional memberships grew, so too did its diplomatic corps,
which became highly professionalized and competent at navigating the
post-war institutions and at using them to advance China's economic
goals, enhance its international status and influence, and advocate for
changes in their procedural and substantive rules. As a result, the PRC
became party to almost all of the U.N.'s treaties and conventions. It is
the second largest contributor to the U.N.'s regular budget and to its
peacekeeping budget, and Chinese diplomats now hold elected positions
on four of its 15 specialized agencies. No other state holds such a position on more than one.[81]

In its role as a permanent member of the U.N. Security Council
China has been sparing but specific with its veto, using it consistently
to reject resolutions it judges to be incompatible with or in outright
violation of Article 2 of the U.N. Charter, which precludes intervention "in matters which are essentially within the domestic jurisdiction
of any state".[82] Since 2000, it also used this rationale to abstain from
or to veto sanctions eight times, but otherwise has supported passage
of 182 sanctions-related resolutions.[83] China has deployed peacekeepers

on more missions than all other permanent members of the Security Council combined—with its participation contingent upon the consent of the host country—and has 8,000 troops in the U.N. peacekeeping standby force.[84]

In matters of trade, with the exception of increases from its trade war with the United States, China has otherwise consistently reduced tariffs since its 2001 accession to the WTO. It also has largely improved the quality of its bilateral and multilateral trade agreements, and has been responsive to conditions placed on its domestic economy by the WTO, IMF, and World Bank.[85] At the WTO, China has used its procedures in a manner commensurate with that of the United States and others—a mix of properly, cleverly, and instrumentally—as a complainant in 23 cases, a respondent in 49, and a third party with an interest in 193 others.[86] Analysts observe that China understands and operates effectively within the WTO's Dispute Settlement Body (DSB) and generally adheres to rulings that run counter to the PRC position.[87]

Its economy, however, is characterized by experts as a non-market hybrid with its market practices combined with government-imposed limitations on data and financial flows, the presence of large state-owned enterprises (SOEs), the use of coercive measures to gain access to companies' technology and intellectual property (often called "forced technology transfer", or FTT), and ample industrial policies. The United States objects to these and other features of China's "party-state capitalism" model because they suppress the quantity and quality of international access to the large Chinese market (digital and actual), advantaging domestic industries locally and, in some cases, internationally.[88] The United States thus far has sought to address these illiberal economic policies not through the WTO but rather through trade mechanisms—unsuccessful attempts first at forging a bilateral deal, and then at finalizing the regional, multilateral Trans-Pacific Partnership (TPP), and then through the imposition of export controls and punitive tariffs.

China also has been accused of currency manipulation, a practice that is prohibited by both the IMF and the WTO but is vexingly difficult to prove. In China's case, and despite being officially designated a manipulator by the Trump administration for six months in 2019–2020, some experts find that the case for intentional malfeasance is at best unclear, and for others it is even considered weak.[89] So too has China been accused of intellectual property theft, conducted through traditional espionage and through FTT, a practice by which China's market access regulations require foreign companies seeking to partner with Chinese firms to share with those firms their intellectual property such as technology, patents, copyrights, and so forth. Espionage of all kinds is not a new phenomenon and is largely considered to be de rigueur in international relations.[90] It is nonetheless illegal, and the advent of cyber tools and techniques makes it more constant and pervasive than ever before. Open-source reporting has identified more than 1,200 separate claims of Chinese industrial espionage conducted against U.S. companies, an accounting that most likely does not capture the true frequency of such efforts.[91] FTT, by comparison, although coercive is not explicitly against the rules, is not uncommon in the developing world, and China has undertaken a series of reforms to restrict such practices.[92]

Far from opting out of or seeking to obstruct or overturn the post–war order's institutions, then, China integrated itself into them and, from there, worked within their procedures to gain and exercise influence. The PRC has also been explicit in expressing its dissatisfaction with rules that it does seek to change. Its role in the creation of new institutions has in fact been described by some analysts as a strategy for strengthening its bargaining position when advocating for reform of the post-war institutions.[93]

China has, however, used military force without U.N. approval on more than one occasion to counter perceived threats to its security and to pursue its own historical claims. It entered the Korean War in opposition to U.N. forces in 1950, arguing that the U.N. action was an unjustified and illegitimate intervention in Korea's domestic affairs and describing U.S. military activity—including the deployment of the Navy's 7th fleet to the Taiwan Strait—as an "invasion" of Asia.[94] In 1962, it fought India over the two countries' disputed border and their respective positions on the status of Tibet. Its border dispute with the Soviet Union escalated to violence in 1969, and in 1979, China invaded Vietnam over yet another border disagreement, this time together with geopolitical concerns about Vietnam's relationship with the USSR, and about Hanoi's intentions toward Chinese ally Cambodia.

Although China has not gone to war since, it has continued to use its military and paramilitary forces to assert its territorial claims, engaging in multiple violent border disputes with India, using aggressive tactics to entrench its own positions and to weaken those of others in East Asia's seas—including the occasional outright use of violence as, for example, its 1988 sinking of two Vietnamese ships in a dispute over possession of Johnson South Reef—and seeking to coerce the self-governed island of Taiwan into unification with the mainland.[95] It has, that is, been especially willing to elevate the role of force in its efforts to firmly etch its own drawing of borders onto internationally accepted maps. In all, the

PRC's record of compliance with the principles and institutions of the post–war order is neither as bad as U.S. discourse would suggest nor as good as Beijing's presentations would contend.

* * *

Notes

1 Michael Schuman, *Superpower Interrupted: The Chinese History of the World* (New York: Hachette Book Group), 2020.
2 Michael Curtis, Ed., *The Great Political Theories, Volume 1* (New York: Avon Books), 1961; Simon Leys, "An Introduction to Confucius", in Simon Leys, Ed., *The Hall of Uselessness: Collected Essays* (New York: NYRB), 2011, pp. 314–328.
3 Ancient China here refers to the period prior to 221 BCE, the time at which China the civilization converted into China a unified empire. For further detail on this period see: Francis Fukuyama, *The Origins of Political Order: From Prehuman Times to the French Revolution* (New York: Farrar, Straus and Giroux), 2011, pp. 97–138.
4 The dao, or "the way", can be interpreted in a number of ways, though all access the idea of creating structure in people's lives. See: Chiao Wei, "Daoism in China", in Max Deeg and Bernhard Scheid, Eds., *Religion in China: Major Concepts and Minority Positions* (Vienna: Austrian Academy of Sciences Press), 2015, pp. 13–28.
5 Evan Osnos, "Confucius Comes Home", *The New Yorker*, January 6, 2014, www.newyorker.com/magazine/2014/01/13/confucius-comes-home; John Dotson, "The Confucian Revival in the Propaganda Narratives of the Chinese Government" (Washington, DC: U.S.-China Economic and Security Review Commission Staff Research Report), July 20, 2011.
6 John King Fairbank, *China: A New History* (Cambridge, MA: Belknap/Harvard University Press, 1992), p. 49; Francis Fukuyama, *The Origins of Political Order: From Prehuman Times to the French Revolution*, p. 111.
7 Karen Armstrong, *The Great Transformation* (New York: Alfred A. Knopf), 2006, pp. 32–36. For a concise explanation of how the mandate of Heaven was understood to operate, see: Martin Jacques, *When China Rules the World: The End of the Western World and the Birth of a New Global Order* (New York: Penguin), 2012 p. 85–86.
8 Karen Armstrong, *The Great Transformation*, pp. 206–208.
9 Ibid., p. 209.
10 Benjamin I. Schwartz, *The World of Thought in Ancient China* (Cambridge, MA: Harvard University Press), 1985, p. 63; Francis Fukuyama, *The Origins of Political Order: From Prehuman Times to the French Revolution*, pp. 119–122.
11 Karen Armstrong, *The Great Transformation*, pp. 331–338.

12 For a brief overview of some of the differences between Confucianism and Legalism, see: Francis Fukuyama, *The Origins of Political Order: From Prehuman Times to the French Revolution*, pp. 119–134. For a lengthy discussion of some of the differences between Confucianism and Legalism, see: Bryan W. Van Norden, *Introduction to Classical Chinese Philosophy* (Indianapolis: Hackett Publishing Company, Inc.), 2011.

13 Although China has no history of democratic modes of thought, much less of practice, even its early metaphysics associated a ruler's legitimacy with the well-being and happiness of the people and established their right to interpret failures to do so as the loss of the mandate of heaven, and therefore to justify deposing him. See: Martin Jacques, *When China Rules the World: The End of the Western World and the Birth of a New Global Order*; Bryan W. Van Norden, *Introduction to Classical Chinese Philosophy*.

14 Francis Fukuyama, *The Origins of Political Order: From Prehuman Times to the French Revolution*, p. 138.

15 During the first millennium of the modern era, China's experience with foreigners was limited to bordering tribal communities and its experience of invasion was by the tribes living on the outer periphery of its understanding of the world. See: Francis Fukuyama, *The Origins of Political Order: From Prehuman Times to the French Revolution*, pp. 292–293; Michael Schuman, *Superpower Interrupted: The Chinese History of the World*, pp. 52–53, 110–116.

16 Michael Schuman, *Superpower Interrupted: The Chinese History of the World*, pp. 144–171.

17 John K. Fairbank, "The Early Treaty System in the Chinese World Order", in John K. Fairbank, Ed., *The Chinese World Order: Traditional China's Foreign Relations* (Cambridge, MA: Harvard University Press), 1968, pp. 257–275.

18 Michael Schuman, *Superpower Interrupted: The Chinese History of the World*, pp. 241–243; Henry Kissinger, *World Order* (New York: Penguin Books), 2015, pp. 218–219.

19 Michael Schuman, *Superpower Interrupted: The Chinese History of the World*, pp. 249–253; Martin Jacques, *When China Rules the World: The End of the Western World and the Birth of a New Global Order*, pp. 71–90.

20 Schwartz in *The Chinese World Order: Traditional China's Foreign Relations*, pp. 276–288.

21 Zheng Wang, "National Humiliation, History Education, and the Politics of Historical Memory: Patriotic Education Campaign in China", *International Studies Quarterly*, Vol. 52, No. 4, 2008, pp. 783–806, www.jstor.org/stable/29734264.

22 Kenneth Lieberthal, *Governing China: From Revolution Through Reform* (New York: W.W. Norton & Company), 2004, 2nd ed., p. 20.

23 In a memorable turn of phrase, China scholar Ken Lieberthal explains that "the reformist medicine finished off the already sick dynastic patient". Ibid., p. 25.

24 Xu Guoqi, *Strangers on the Western Front: Chinese Workers in the Great War* (Cambridge, MA: Harvard University Press, 2011).

25 Diana Lary, "China and Japan at War: Suffering and Survival, 1937–1945", *The Asia Pacific Journal*, Vol. 8, No. 48, No. 2, November 29, 2010, pp. 1–8.

26 Henry Kissinger, *World Order*, p. 221; Elizabeth C. Economy, *The World According to China* (Medford: Polity Press), 2022, p. 172; David L. Bosco, *Five to Rule Them All: The UN Security Council and the Making of the Modern World* (Oxford: Oxford University Press), 2009, pp. 24–54.

27 Allen Carlson, *Unifying China, Integrating with the World: Securing Chinese Sovereignty in the Reform Era* (Stanford, CA: Stanford University Press), 2005, pp. 37–43.

28 Samuel S. Kim, "The People's Republic of China in the United Nations: A Preliminary Analysis", *World Politics*, Vol. 26, No. 3, 2011, pp. 299–330, https://doi.org/10.2307/2009932.

29 Byron S. Weng, "Communist China's Changing Attitudes toward the United Nations", *International Organization*, Vol. 20, No. 4, 1966, pp. 677–704, www.jstor.org/stable/2705736.

30 Evan Luard, "China and the United Nations", *International Affairs*, Royal Institute of International Affairs, Vol. 47, No. 4, 1971, pp. 729–744, https://doi.org/10.2307/2625680; Suisheng Zhao, *The Dragon Roars Back: Transformational Leaders and Dynamics of Chinese Foreign Policy* (Stanford, CA: Stanford University Press), 2023, pp. 23–49.

31 Samuel S. Kim, *China, the United Nations and World Order* (Princeton, NJ: Princeton University Press), 1979, Chapter 2, www.jstor.org/stable/j.ctt13x16fn, "Global Politics in the General Assembly" pp. 97–177; Zhongjun Niu, "A Historical Overview of China-U.N. Relations", *Journal of Asia-Pacific Studies*, Vol. 30, January 2018, pp. 65–76, https://core.ac.uk/download/pdf/286958607.pdf.

32 Michael Schuman, *Superpower Interrupted: The Chinese History of the World*, pp. 292–294; Evan Osnos, "The Cost of the Cultural Revolution, Fifty Years Later", *The New Yorker*, May 6, 2016, www.newyorker.com/news/daily-comment/the-cost-of-the-cultural-revolution-fifty-years-later.

33 Orville Schell and John Delury, *Wealth and Power: China's Long March to the Twenty-First Century* (New York: Random House), 2014, p. 328.

34 "Our Work in all Fields Should Contribute to the Building of Socialism with Chinese Characteristics", Deng Xiaoping, talk with leading members of the State Planning commission, the State Economic Commission and departments in charge of agriculture, January 12, 1983; Ibid., pp. 279–283; Stephen Roach, *Accidental Conflict; America, China, and the Clash of False Narratives* (London: Yale University Press), 2022, pp. 213–219.

35 Peter Martin, *China's Civilian Army: The Making of Wolf Warrior Diplomacy* (New York: Oxford University Press), 2021.

36 Tianbiao Zhu, "Rethinking Import-Substituting Industrialization: Development Strategies and Institutions in Taiwan and China", Research Paper 2006/076 (Helsinki: UNU-WIDER), 2006, www.wider.unu.edu/publication/rethinking-import-substituting-industrialization.

37 "How Influential is China in the World Trade Organization" (Washington, DC: CSIS), *ChinaPower*, accessed September 2023, https://chinapower.csis.org/china-world-trade-organization-wto/.

38 Penelope B. Prime, "China Joins the WTO: How, Why and What Now?", *Business Economics*, Vol. XXXVII, No. 2, April 2002, pp. 26–32; Nicholas R. Lardy, "Issues in China's WTO Accession" (Washington, DC: The Brookings Institution), May 9, 2001, www.brookings.edu/articles/issues-in-chinas-wto-accession/.

39 Allen Carlson, *Unifying China, Integrating with the World*, (Stanford, CA: Stanford University Press), 2005, Chapter 6, "Economic Sovereignty: Accelerating Integration and Accumulating Obligations", pp. 184–223.

40 Zhongjun Niu, "A Historical Overview of China-U.N. Relations.

41 Ibid.

42 Andrew J. Nathan, "The Tiananmen Papers", *Foreign Affairs*, January 1, 2001, www.foreignaffairs.com/articles/asia/2001-01-01/tiananmen-papers.

43 James B. Steinberg, "What Went Wrong? U.S.-China Relations from Tiananmen to Trump", *Texas National Security Review*, Vol. 3, No. 1, 2019/2020, pp. 65–76, https://tnsr.org/2020/01/what-went-wrong-u-s-china-relations-from-tiananmen-to-trump/.

44 Nancy Bernkopf Tucker, "A Precarious Balance: Clinton and China", *Current History*, Vol. 97, No. 620, 1998, pp. 243–249, www.jstor.org/stable/45317828.

45 The carriers did not go into or through the Strait itself, but remained in the Philippine Sea. David M. Lampton, "China and Clinton's America: Have They Learned Anything?" *Asian Survey*, Vol. 37, No. 12, 1997, pp. 1099–1118, https://doi.org/10.2307/2645760.

46 Ann Kent, "China's Participation in International Organisations", in Yongjin Zhang and Greg Austin, Eds., *Power and Responsibility in Chinese Foreign Policy* (Canberra: ANU Press), 2013, pp. 132–166, www.jstor.org/stable/j.ctt5vj73b.

47 Zhongjun Niu, "A Historical Overview of China-U.N. Relations".

48 "China's Response to the Global Financial Crisis: Implications for U.S. Economic Interests" (Washington, DC: Congressional Research Service), March 3, 1999, www.everycrsreport.com/files/19990303_98-220_59def0ce26c6f54aab46514fa8663eb8ac2c1951.pdf.

49 Yong Deng, "Hegemon on the Offensive: Chinese Perspectives on U. S. Global Strategy", *Political Science Quarterly*, Vol. 116, No. 3, 2001, pp. 343–365, https://doi.org/10.2307/798020.

50 Jacques deLisle, "9/11 and U.S.-China Relations", *Foreign Policy Research Institute*, September 3, 2011, www.fpri.org/article/2011/09/911-and-u-s-china-relations/.

51 "1992–2018 The U.S. Financial Crisis" (Washington, DC: Council on Foreign Relations), accessed August 2024, www.cfr.org/timeline/us-financial-crisis.

52 Although the "pivot to Asia" was a feature in pronouncements by the administrations of both Barack Obama and Donald Trump, it has only meaningfully become a feature of policy in 2022–2023, as the Biden administration has expanded U.S. access to basing in the Philippines. Stacie Pettyjohn, "U.S. Global Defense Posture, 1783–2011" (Santa Monica, CA: RAND Corporation), 2012, www.rand.org/pubs/monographs/MG1244.html; Andrew Yeo and Michael E. O'Hanlon, "Geostrategic Competition and Overseas Basing in East Asia and the First Island Chain" (Washington, DC: The Brookings Institution), February 2023, www.brookings.edu/wp-content/uploads/2023/02/FP_20230207_east_asia_basing_ohanlon_yeo.pdf; Wee Sui-Lee, "U.S. to Boost Military Role in the Philippines in Push to Counter China", *The New York Times*, February 3, 2023, www.nytimes.com/2023/02/01/world/asia/philippines-united-states-military-bases.html.

53 Kenneth G. Lieberthal, "The American Pivot to Asia" (Washington, DC: The Brookings Institution), December 21, 2011, www.brookings.edu/articles/the-american-pivot-to-asia/.

54 Rush Doshi, *The Long Game: China's Strategy to Displace American Order* (New York: Oxford University Press), 2021.

55 Chris Buckley, "Behind Public Assurances, Xi Jinping Spread Grim Views on U.S.", *The New York Times*, November 13, 2023, www.nytimes.com/2023/11/13/world/asia/china-xi-asia-pacific-summit.html; Suisheng Zhao, *The Dragon Roars Back: Transformational Leaders and Dynamics of Chinese Foreign Policy*, pp. 154–173.

56 Kevin Rudd, "The World According to Xi Jinping: What China's Ideologue in Chief Really Believes", *Foreign Affairs*, October 10, 2022, www.foreignaffairs.com/china/world-according-xi-jinping-china-ideologue-kevin-rudd?gad=1&gclid=Cj0KCQjwxYOiBhC9ARIsANiEIfZCuPP2OkjbynQIykptx9Og4FLJMmuPBp-kj3DC7b2tQCQ1pZY8-rYaAnhWEALw_wcB.

57 Because BRI is, fundamentally, a means through which it pursues economic development through the mechanisms of globalization, it is not possible to arrive at an accurate estimate of total spending. Attempts hazarded in the late 2010s range from $1 trillion to $8 trillion. See: Jane Perlez and Yufan Huang, "Behind China's $1 Trillion Plan to Shake up the Economic Order", *The New York Times*, May 13, 2013, www.nytimes.com/2017/05/13/business/china-railway-one-belt-one-road-1-trillion-plan.html; "China's Belt and Road Initiative in the Global Trade, Investment and Finance Landscape", OECD Business and Finance Outlook, 2018, www.oecd.org/finance/Chinas-Belt-and-Road-Initiative-in-the-global-trade-investment-and-finance-landscape.pdf; Bates Gill, *Daring to Struggle: China's Global Ambitions under Xi Jinping* (New York: Oxford University Press), 2022, pp. 87–90.

58 Separate from BRI, in 2020, China signed the Regional Comprehensive Economic Partnership, which has been described as "the
largest free trade agreement in history", with 14 other Asia Pacific
nations. Peter A. Petri and Michael Plummer, "RCEP: A New
Trade Agreement that Will Shape Global Economics and Politics"
(Washington, DC: The Brookings Institution), November 16, 2020,
www.brookings.edu/articles/rcep-a-new-trade-agreement-that-
will-shape-global-economics-and-politics/; "Xi's New Global Development Initiative" (Washington, DC: CSIS), September 12, 2022,
www.csis.org/events/xis-new-global-development-initiative.

59 Made in China 2025 followed after implementation of prior industrial policies focused on the technology sector, notably the Medium-
and Long-Term Program for Science and Technology Development
(2006) and the "strategic emerging industries initiative" (2010).
Both are described clearly and concisely in: Arthur R. Kroeber, "The
Economic Origins of US-China Strategic Competition", in Evan S.
Medeiros, Ed., *Cold Rivals: The New Era of US-China Strategic
Competition* (Washington, DC: Georgetown University Press), 2023,
pp. 172–204.

60 Kristen A. Cordell, "The Evolving Relationship between the International Development Architecture and China's Belt and Road" (Washington, DC: The Brookings Institution), October 2020, www.brookings.
edu/articles/the-evolving-relationship-between-the-international-
development-architecture-and-chinas-belt-and-road/; Christina Lu,
"China's Belt and Road to Nowhere", *Foreign Policy*, February 13,
2023, https://foreignpolicy.com/2023/02/13/china-belt-and-road-
initiative-infrastructure-development-geopolitics/; Rush Doshi, *The
Long Game: China's Strategy to Displace American Order*, 2021
pp. 241–246; "Transcript of Attorney General Barr's Remarks on
China Policy at the Gerald R. Ford Presidential Museum", Grand
Rapids MI, Friday July 17, 2020, www.justice.gov/opa/speech/
transcript-attorney-general-barr-s-remarks-china-policy-gerald-
r-ford-presidential-museum; Dylan Gerstel, "It's a (Dept) Trap!
Managing China-IMF Cooperation across the Belt and Road"
(Washington, DC: CSIS), October 17, 2018, www.csis.org/analysis/
its-debt-trap-managing-china-imf-cooperation-across-belt-and-road.

61 Kurt M. Campbell and Ely Ratner, "The China Reckoning: How
Beijing Defied American Expectations", *Foreign* Affairs, March/
April 2018, www.foreignaffairs.com/articles/china/2018-02-13/china-
reckoning; James McBride and Andrew Chatzky, "Is 'Made in China
2025' a Threat to Global Trade?" (New York: Council on Foreign Relations), May 13, 2019, www.cfr.org/backgrounder/made-china-202
5-threat-global-trade#chapter-title-0-4; Brad Setser, "U.S.-China Trade
War: How We Got Here" (New York: Council on Foreign Relations),
July 9, 2018, www.cfr.org/blog/us-china-trade-war-how-we-got-here?
utm_medium=email&utm_source=dailybrief&utm_content=
071118&sp_mid=56974456&sp_rid=ai5lbGxpb3QubWNicmlkZU
BnbWFpbC5jb20S1.

62 Ellis Joffe, "Shaping China's Next Generation of Military Leaders" (Carlisle: Strategic Studies Institute, US Army War College), 2008; Brian R. Moore and Renato R. Barreda, "China's PLA Gets Smarter and Bigger, Faster, Stronger", *Foreign Policy*, August 9, 2016; "Chinese Military Set Up Joint Operations Command Center: Sources", *The Japan Times*, August 7, 2014, www.japantimes.co.jp/news/2014/08/07/asia-pacific/chinese-military-set-joint-operations-command-center-sources/#.WgIhHRNSyRs; Patricia Kim, "Understanding China's Military Expansion", Pacific-Council on International Policy, prepared statement for the House Permanent Select committee on Intelligence of the US House of Representatives, May 17, 2018, www.pacificcouncil.org/newsroom/understanding-china%E2%80%99s-military-expansion; "China's Military: The People's Liberation Army (PLA)", Congressional Research Service, R46808, June 4, 2021, https://crsreports.congress.gov/product/pdf/R/R46808.

63 "China's Military Spending (1989–2011, in US\$ billion and % of GDP)", (Brussels: European Parliamentary Research Service), accessed August 2024, https://epthinktank.eu/2013/04/16/chinas-military-rise/china1/; Matthew P. Funaiole et al., "Understanding China's 2021 Defense Budget" (Washington, DC: Center for Strategic and International Studies), March 5, 2021, www.csis.org/analysis/understanding-chinas-2021-defense-budget.

64 Kevin L. Pollpeter, Michael S. Chase, and Eric Heginbotham, "The Creation of the PLA Strategic Support Force and Its Implications for Chinese Military Space Operations" (Santa Monica, CA: RAND Corporation), 2017; John Costello and Joe McReynolds, "China's Strategic Support Force: A Force for a New Era", *China Strategic Perspectives,* Center for the Study of Chinese Military Affairs Institute for National Strategic Studies, No. 13, October 2018, https://ndupress.ndu.edu/Portals/68/Documents/stratperspective/china/china-perspectives_13.pdf.

65 Frederic Wehrey and Sandy Alkoutami, "China's Balancing Act in Libya" (Washington, DC: Carnegie Endowment for International Peace), May 10, 2020, https://carnegieendowment.org/2020/05/10/china-s-balancing-act-in-libya-pub-81757.

66 Michael Tanchum, "China's New Military Base in Africa: What it Means for Europe and America" (New York: European Council on Foreign Relations), December 14, 2021, https://ecfr.eu/article/chinas-new-military-base-in-africa-what-it-means-for-europe-and-america/.

67 Alison A. Kaufman, "China's Participation in Anti-Piracy Operations off the Horn of Africa: Drivers and Implications" (Washington, DC: Center for Naval Analyses, China Studies), July 2009, www.cna.org/reports/2009/D0020834.A1.pdf.

68 Bonnie Glaser, "Why Did China Build and Militarize Islands in the South China Sea, and Should the United States Care?", in Maria Adele Carrai, Jennifer Rudolph, and Michael Szonyi, Eds., *The*

China Questions 2: Critical Insights into US-China Relations (Cambridge: Harvard University Press), 2022, Chapter 25, pp. 230–237.

69 Derek Grossman and Logan Ma, "A Short History of China's Fishing Militia and What it May Tell Us" (Santa Monica, CA: RAND Corporation), April 6, 2022, www.rand.org/blog/2020/04/a-short-history-of-chinas-fishing-militia-and-what.html.

70 Matthew Reynolds and Matthew P. Goodman, "China's Economic Coercion: Lessons from Lithuania" (Washington, DC: CSIS), May 6, 2022, www.csis.org/analysis/chinas-economic-coercion-lessons-lithuania.

71 "Statement of the Government of the People's Republic of China" (Washington, DC: The Wilson Center), October 16, 1964, https://digitalarchive.wilsoncenter.org/document/statement-government-peoples-republic-china.

72 Fiona S. Cunningham, "The Unknowns about China's Nuclear Modernization Program" (Washington, DC: Arms Control Association), June 2023, www.armscontrol.org/act/2023-06/features/unknowns-about-chinas-nuclear-modernization-program; Kelsey Davenport, "Nuclear Weapons: Who Has What at a Glance" (Washington, DC: Arms Control Association), June 2023, www.armscontrol.org/factsheets/Nuclearweaponswhohaswhat.

73 Quoted in Pan Zhenqiang, "China's No First Use of Nuclear Weapons", in Li Bin and Tong Zhao, Eds., *Understanding Chinese Nuclear Thinking* (Washington, DC: Carnegie Endowment for International Peace), 2016, www.jstor.org/stable/resrep26903.7.

74 "Military and Security Developments Involving the People's Republic of China" (Washington, DC: United States Department of Defense), 2023, pp. 51–78.

75 Chris Buckley, "Fear and Ambition Propel Xi's Nuclear Acceleration", *The New York Times*, February 4, 2024, www.nytimes.com/2024/02/04/world/asia/china-nuclear-missiles.html.

76 M. Taylor Fravel, Henrik Stalhane Hiim, and Magnus Langset Troan, "China's Misunderstood Nuclear Expansion", *Foreign Affairs*, November 10, 2023, www.foreignaffairs.com/china/chinas-misunderstood-nuclear-expansion?utm_medium=newsletters&utm_source=fatoday&utm_campaign=China%E2%80%99s%20Misunderstood%20Nuclear%20Expansion&utm_content=20231110&utm_term=FA%20Today%20-%20112017; See also: M. Taylor Fravel, "Deterring a Cross-Strait Conflict: Beijing's Assessment of Evolving U.S. Strategy" (Washington, DC: Center for Strategic and International Studies), *Interpret: China*, March 29, 2023, https://interpret.csis.org/deterring-a-cross-strait-conflict-beijings-assessment-of-evolving-u-s-strategy/.

77 Rush Doshi, *The Long Game: China's Strategy to Displace American Order*, p. 113.

78 Eric Helleiner, *Forgotten Foundations of Bretton Woods* (Ithaca, NY: Cornell University Press), 2014, Chapter 6; David L. Bosco, *Five to Rule Them All: The UN Security Council and the Making of the Modern World*, pp. 24–54.

79 The PRC joined the World Bank and the IMF in 1976.
80 Robert D. Williams, "International Law with Chinese Characteristics: Beijing and the 'Rules-Based' Global Order" (Washington, DC: The Brookings Institution), October 2020, www.brookings.edu/wp-content/uploads/2020/10/FP_20201012_international_law_china_williams.pdf.
81 Courtney Fung and Shing-Hon Lam, "China Already Leads 4 of the 15 U.N. Specialized Agencies—and Is Aiming for a 5th", *The Washington Post*, March 3, 2020, www.washingtonpost.com/politics/2020/03/03/china-already-leads-4-15-un-specialized-agencies-is-aiming-5th/; Courtney J. Fung and Shing-hon Lam, "Mixed Report Card: China's Influence at the United Nations" (Sydney: Lowy Institute), December 18, 2022.
82 As of July 2023 China had used the veto 17 times.
83 "Is China Contributing to the United Nations' Mission?", *China Power* (Washington, DC: CSIS), accessed July 2, 2023, https://chinapower.csis.org/china-un-mission/.
84 Suisheng Zhao, *The Dragon Roars Back: Transformational Leaders and Dynamics of Chinese Foreign Policy*, p. 236; Jeffrey Feltman, "China's Expanding Influence at the United Nations" (Washington, DC: The Brookings Institution), September 2020, www.brookings.edu/articles/chinas-expanding-influence-at-the-united-nations-and-how-the-united-states-should-react/.
85 Suisheng Zhao, *The Dragon Roars Back: Transformational Leaders and Dynamics of Chinese Foreign Policy*; Michael Mazarr, Timothy R. Heath, and Astrid Stuth Cevallos, "China and the International Order" (Santa Monica, CA: RAND Corporation), 2018, www.rand.org/pubs/research_reports/RR2423.html.
86 The United States has been a complainant in 124 cases, a respondent in 158, and third party to 175.
87 Robert D. Williams, "International Law with Chinese Characteristics: Beijing and the 'Rules-Based' Global Order".
88 Margaret Pearson, Meg Rithmire, and Kellee S. Tsai, "Party-State Capitalism in China", *Current History*, Vol. 120, No. 827, September 2021, pp. 207–213, www.hbs.edu/ris/Publication%20Files/CURH120827_01_Pearson_4ea34a0b-21d5-45af-a51a-c938eeeb6380.pdf; Joshua P. Meltzer, "China's Digital Services Trade and Data Governance: How Should the United States Respond?" (Washington, DC: The Brookings Institution), October 2020, www.brookings.edu/articles/chinas-digital-services-trade-and-data-governance-how-should-the-united-states-respond/; David Dollar and Ryan Hass, "Getting the China Challenge Right" (Washington, DC: The Brookings Institution), January 25, 2021, www.brookings.edu/articles/getting-the-china-challenge-right/#challenge; Keyu Jin, *The New China Playbook: Beyond Socialism and Capitalism* (New York: Viking), 2023, p. 7; DiPippo Gerard, Ilaria Mazzocco, and Scott Kennedy, "Red Ink: Estimating Chinese Industrial Policy Spending in Comparative Perspective" (Washington,

DC: CSIS), May 2022, www.csis.org/analysis/red-ink-estimating-chinese-industrial-policy-spending-comparative-perspective; Stephen Roach, *Accidental Conflict; America, China, and the Clash of False Narratives*, pp. 87–92.

89 Michael W. Klein, "What You May not Know about China and Currency Manipulation" (Washington, DC: The Brookings Institution), May 22, 2015, www.brookings.edu/articles/what-you-may-not-know-about-china-and-currency-manipulation/; Brad W. Setser, "Is China Manipulating its Currency?" (New York: Council on Foreign Relations), August 8, 2019, www.cfr.org/in-brief/china-manipulating-its-currency.

90 William J. Burns, "Spycraft and Statecraft: Transforming the CIA for an Age of Competition", *Foreign Affairs*, January 30, 2024, www.foreignaffairs.com/united-states/cia-spycraft-and-statecraft-william-burns; James Mulvenon explains, however, that and why the "United States government, probably alone among nationals governments, does not engage in commercial economic espionage on behalf of its companies", James Mulvenon, "Nontraditional Security Competition", in Medeiros, *Cold Rivals*, pp. 271–272.

91 "Survey of Chinese Espionage in the United States Since 2000" (Washington, DC: CSIS), accessed July 3, 2023, www.csis.org/programs/strategic-technologies-program/archives/survey-chinese-espionage-united-states-2000; James Mulvenon, "Nontraditional Security Competition", pp. 264–266.

92 Alan O. Sykes, "The Law and Economics of 'Forced' Technology Transfer and its Implications for Trade and Investment Policy (and the U.S.-China Trade War)", *Journal of Legal Analysis*, Vol. 13, No. 1, 2021, pp. 127–171, https://academic.oup.com/jla/article/13/1/127/6180583; Stephen Roach, *Accidental Conflict; America, China, and the Clash of False Narratives*, pp. 81–84; Jyhan Lee, "Forced Technology Transfer in the Case of China", *Boston University Journal of Science & Technology Law*, Vol. 26, No. 2, 2020, pp. 324–352, www.bu.edu/jostl/files/2020/08/3-Lee.pdf.

93 Evan A. Feigenbaum, "Reluctant Stakeholder: Why China's Highly Strategic Brand of Revisionism Is More Challenging than Washington Thinks", *Macro Polo*, April 27, 2018, https://macropolo.org/analysis/reluctant-stakeholder-why-chinas-highly-strategic-brand-of-revisionism-is-more-challenging-than-washington-thinks/.

94 Henry Kissinger, *On China* (New York: Penguin Books), 2012, p. 130.

95 Hao Yufan and Zhai Zhihai. "China's Decision to Enter the Korean War: History Revisited", *The China Quarterly*, Vol. 121, 1990, pp. 94–115, www.jstor.org/stable/654064.

5

THE COMPETITION FOR CONTROL

* * *

Much of the U.S. national security community—across political parties and over two consecutive but very different presidential administrations—has adopted a narrative about U.S.–China competition that is as insistent about America's attachment to the post–war order as it is about China's intent to supplant it with a less legitimate and more dangerous one. More than this, it is a narrative that presents the post–war order as a structure designed to propagate economic and political liberalism and that places that order in stark contrast with an alternative defined by the most illiberal interpretation of China's internal politics and external ambitions. It argues that an order structured to reflect the U.S. approach to order will be "free, open, prosperous, and secure", while one that reflects China's approach to order will be self-serving in its management of international finance and trade, menacing to the well-being of individuals, and threatening to the territorial sovereignty of states.[1]

For its part, the CCP has increased the volume on its longstanding objections not to the fact, but to the operation, of the post–war order. Much of this is grounded in China's perceptions of historical injustice and the system's accommodation of U.S. hegemony, the most aggravating element of which is its efforts to elevate the rights of individuals over the prerogatives of national governments—efforts enabled by substantial U.S. military presence around the world, including in East Asia. Official pronouncements, including many of Xi Jinping's speeches, have called the U.S. approach a Cold War hangover that, they say, can only produce dangerous "confrontation between blocs" and that "history has proved time and again . . . only invites catastrophic consequences". Beijing counters that this approach to interstate relations should be renounced in favor of its own, which it describes as prioritizing a "true multilateralism" that promotes a global economy characterized by transparency,

DOI: 10.4324/9781032723358-5

openness, and "fairness and justice". Such an order would create international stability by forming rules that address the "legitimate security concerns of all countries" in ways that do not "reject, threaten or intimidate others" using "unilateral sanctions, and long-arm jurisdiction" but rather through "dialogue, consultation and other peaceful means".[2]

The shared understanding that the United States and China do have about international order is that they are in competition about it and that both are endeavoring to exert control over its terms. The policies they are undertaking in that pursuit—to increase their share of global commerce, to lead advances in science and technology, to extend and expand their diplomatic influence, and to develop robust military capabilities—are affecting all parts of the globe, from the Blue Pacific to Africa to the Arctic, and everywhere in between.

The United States and the Post–War Order

It is becoming increasingly difficult to describe U.S. grand strategy—the combination and interaction of its economic and foreign policies (diplomatic and military) for purposes of promoting U.S. prosperity and security—as consistent with, much less as guided by, the precepts of free trade multilateralism. Motivated in part by the genuine belief that the operation of free trade has been harmful to some sectors of the U.S. economy, and in part by concern about the current trade regime's distribution of benefits between the United States and China, the United States has imposed tariffs and export restrictions, is increasingly unwilling to enter into free trade agreements, and has provided substantial subsidies and tax credits to domestic industries. While the Biden Administration sought to reassure the world that "U.S. military power must be our tool of last resort, not our first", it nonetheless initiated and implemented what some call a "muscular", and others a "militarized", foreign policy agenda.[3] So too does the United States in one moment concede that the post–war order does not require "that governments and societies everywhere must be remade in America's image" and in another assert that competition over global order is nothing less than a battle between authoritarianism and democracy.[4]

Free Trade

During the 2020 presidential election cycle, candidate Biden went to great pains to highlight the wide and deep differences of style and of substance between himself and the incumbent President Donald Trump. Many of these differences translated after the election into changes in policy. In the ten days after inauguration, Biden went about undoing much of what his predecessor had done and, conversely, doing what he believed Trump ought to have done but didn't do on issues from COVID to climate.[5] He did not, however, undo the Trump administration's posture on trade with China, leaving in place tariffs on thousands of Chinese goods ranging from solar panels to food to furniture.[6]

The Biden administration in fact added restrictions that, while limited in the specific items affected, are potentially unlimited in the effect they will have on the Chinese economy. This is by design. U.S. policymakers have concluded that surpassing China in technological innovation is essential to acquiring and sustaining geopolitical advantage, and military-technological advantage in particular. So, in October 2022, the United States put its thumb on China's ability to develop the next generation of advanced computer-based capabilities by imposing a set of extensive controls on China's access to designs, tools, products, and personnel used in the manufacture of the most advanced semiconductors. This was followed in August 2023 with regulations that preclude U.S. individuals and entities from making financial investments in certain segments of China's high technology industry.[7]

These China-specific measures are being accompanied by and reflected in the de-liberalizing of U.S. trade relationships more broadly. In April 2023, the Biden administration announced that the United States would now forego multilateral agreements characterized by low tariffs, and would instead look to enter into smaller plurilateral arrangements that include conditions on corporate taxation, environmental protections, and labor requirements.[8] This shift was enacted concurrently with sizable government interventions in the U.S. economy, most especially in industries the United States believes will be the foundations of economic growth and productivity over the next decade and beyond. Their purpose is to encourage domestic technological advances, primarily in computing, climate, and biotechnology, and to increase the resilience of U.S. supply chains in part by reducing the presence of Chinese companies in them.

Regardless of their outcome, these policies reinforce the CCP's perception that the United States intends to stymie China's economic growth and national development, and they force hard choices on U.S. allies and partners. The CHIPS and Science Act of 2022, for example, pairs domestic investments in pure research and in workforce development with subsidies and tax credits to incentivize U.S. and foreign companies to manufacture semiconductors within the United States. It makes receipt of those subsidies and tax credits, however, contingent on compliance with restrictions on what those companies build and source in China. This intensifies the entanglement of economic policies with political and security relationships, creating considerable dilemmas for business leaders and policymakers as they consider their interests in and exposures to the United States, on the one hand, and China, on the other.[9] The Inflation Reduction Act of 2022 similarly creates protections for U.S. clean energy industries, though in this case in ways that important European partners object are unfair and that are being used to justify "the need for Europe to respond with its own subsidy package".[10]

The United States explains this retrenchment from free trade and the stresses it creates in its relationships with even long-time trade partners as a response to an international environment in which the gains of liberalization and the benefits of institutionalized multilateral economic regimes no longer outweigh their costs and risks.[11] Government officials and many analysts and commentators argue that this is the necessary response to market forces that have harmed U.S. workers, to the risk China poses to national security, and to China's non-market economy, which members of the Biden administration described as having "all but broken the WTO".[12]

Although there is indeed unhappiness within the United States and other nations that the WTO's rules do not adequately account for China's non-market hybridism, little progress has been made in adapting its rules. There are specific areas of contention—over how states are given "developing country" status and its attendant rights and exemptions, for example, and over the composition of the body's Appellate Board. It is the United States, however, that is currently blocking appointments to fill Board vacancies and thereby creating paralysis in the dispute review process. So too, despite repeated affirmations of commitment to the WTO, is U.S. ambivalence evident in its rejections of the organization's rulings—as, for example, against its steel and aluminum tariffs—on the grounds that the United States "will not cede decision-making over its essential security to WTO panels".[13]

As the United States reconfigures its approach to international trade, it also is changing the ways and places in which it engages developing economies. Here, it will continue to work through the World Bank, but not exclusively. As part of the G7 grouping of wealthy democracies, for example, it has committed to participate in efforts to restructure debt and to finance projects that, among other things, improve recipient nations' health and technology infrastructure and advance gender equality.[14]

Independent of these multilateral initiatives the Biden administration's FY2024 budget increased its development aid request by 16% over the preceding year with $11 billion allocated specifically for engagement with Pacific Island nations. These are countries, like Tonga and Palau, with which China has been engaging on economic and security concerns for years, and that therefore now are being treated as strategically significant to the United States after it "largely abandoned the region" during the post–Cold War period.[15] These funds constitute a U.S. attempt to "out-compete the PRC . . . to deliver the quality, high-standard infrastructure that countries seek across the Indo-Pacific region".[16] This explanation of the timing and purposes of U.S. attention to these nations is, unfortunately, quite honest. The United States does have a quality and standards advantage, but it is one that it hasn't used to good effect for decades. The result is that it is chasing China's tail when it comes to engaging with these nations and, more broadly, when it comes to the design and implementation of a comprehensive and effective strategy for investing in developing economies around the world.

The drive to "out-compete" China is therefore generating productive and destructive energies in U.S. international economic policy. It is producing proper, albeit belated, investments in domestic infrastructure and R&D, attention to development finance, and interest in deepening U.S. relationships with developing economies. It also, however, is superseding prior and productive U.S. attachment to the purposes and practices of free trade. This places strain on U.S. relationships with long-standing trading partners, complicates efforts to acquire new ones, and stresses the economic foundations of the post–war order.[17]

Multilateralism

The primary political foundation of the post–war order was its use of multilateral mechanisms to reduce the likelihood and incidence of war. The economic institutions were to be focused on minimizing and ameliorating tensions caused by commerce, and the United Nations was to be devoted to monitoring irritants in interstate relations and imposing limitations on the use of force to resolve them. The goal was not to preclude self-defense or to eliminate state militaries. It was, rather, in its most humble rendering, to reduce the role of force in the conduct of interstate relations. In its most grandiloquent rendering, the U.N. was to "spell the end of the system of unilateral action, the exclusive alliances, the spheres of influence, the balances of power, and all the other expedients that have been tried for centuries—and have always failed".[18]

The Biden administration's foreign policy was out of alignment with both the minimalist and the maximalist rendering of this goal. Although it dispatched an experienced diplomat to represent the United States as

Ambassador to the United Nations, and President Biden twice gave supportive speeches at the annual meeting of the General Assembly, U.S. foreign policy patently did not reduce but instead elevated the role of force in its foreign policy.

The United States now is energetically implementing two successive, highly confrontational, and expensive national defense strategies (NDS). These have their origins in concern about a conflict over Taiwan—and roots in the Obama administration's designs on "pivoting" U.S. attention toward Asia—but are designed to correct what the Department of Defense fears is a waning of U.S. military superiority in East Asia more generally. The 2018 NDS made public the Department's conclusion that China's military advances had made a U.S. defeat of the PLA in a war over Taiwan uncertain. The 2022 NDS carried that concern further and oriented the Department around the mission of prevailing in a war with China in the Western Pacific.[19] Execution of these strategies has included large investments in warfighting assets and platforms ranging from fleets of small uncrewed drones and submersibles, to Navy destroyers and fighter aircraft, to hypersonic missiles. These investments are meant to "counter adversary threats in the Indo-Pacific region", the swathe of water that stretches "from our Pacific coastline to the Indian Ocean".[20]

The United States is pairing this investment in U.S. warfighting power with the enlargement of its military relationships and overseas activities. In the broadly conceived Indo-Pacific region, it has set about creating new security alignments designed to reinforce perceptions of its intention to maintain U.S. freedom of action. It has intensified its security engagements with India, Japan, and Australia via the Quadrilateral Security Dialogue (the Quad). It created a new Western Pacific-oriented military submarine coalition with the United Kingdom and Australia (AUKUS). It is building up its warfighting footprint on Guam and in other Pacific territories, and it is making new forward-rotation, basing access, and logistics agreements with Australia, the Philippines, South Korea, and India.[21]

The Biden administration presented these changes as necessary to defend a "free and open Indo-Pacific" against China's growing military power and, in particular, to deter a Chinese attack on Taiwan, efforts into which the United States has lobbied to enlist not only allies and partners within the Indo-Pacific but also its far-distant European allies in NATO.[22] Inside the United States, arguments for investing in and emplacing even more of its own warfighting assets in the Indo-Pacific for these purposes are increasing in frequency, intensity, and purchase among policymakers, most especially in Congress.[23]

Worryingly, these energies are also beginning to propel debate about U.S. nuclear strategy. In 2023, the Strategic Posture Commission—a group charged with assessing U.S. nuclear strategy—rightly recommended completion of already-programmed efforts to ensure the U.S. nuclear enterprise can function safely and effectively into the future. This was paired, however, with recommendations that the United States add investments that will enable it to expand its stockpile in the future beyond the approximately 1,800 nuclear warheads it currently deploys and the additional 3,400 or so it maintains in storage. The report also urges the United States to "address the need" to deploy nuclear forces in "the Asia-Pacific theater" beyond its existing in-region presence of dual-capable and low yield assets.[24]

The Commission's rationale for these recommendations is based largely on the assumption, about which there is no expert consensus, that China has "decided to change the role of nuclear weapons in its national security strategy (e.g., adopting an expanded theater nuclear war-fighting role), in anticipation of a conflict over Taiwan and perhaps in pursuit of its broader national objectives".[25] These recommendations do not address concerns about how current U.S. warfighting preparations in the Indo-Pacific factor into China's strategic calculus, or about the likelihood that growth in the U.S. nuclear stockpile might only precipitate similar growth in that of China and Russia—which would make it progressively more, not less, difficult to deter a Russia-China nuclear alliance, as the Commission suggests the United States will need to be prepared do. The report also does not make clear what number or magnitude of nuclear weapons the United States will need to be able to detonate before possession or launch of additional warheads becomes a meaningless gesture.

Nonetheless, there is considerable and still growing momentum behind measures to reassert U.S. conventional and nuclear military dominance in the Indo-Pacific. This is understandable insofar as the United States is accustomed to wielding its military to influence others. It is a habit, however, that reveals the United States has not yet accommodated itself to the fact that warfighting preparedness is not afforded as much importance or priority by other regional and global actors as it is by the United States. Military efforts to exercise control over regional dynamics thus are problematic not only because they break faith with the post-war order but also because they may not have the desired effect. To the contrary, overweighting traditional military engagement relative to addressing other security and economic priorities leaves room for China to draw unfavorable comparisons with its own foreign policy agenda.

China and the Post–War Order

Serious and sensitive observers of modern China describe today's society as one in which its history of civilizational glory, accomplishment, and loss are far from forgotten or elided. To the contrary, they argue that the generational lessons of the century of humiliation—Western subjugation of China's great cultural and intellectual achievements and the cleaving off of pieces of its homeland—continue to shape the people's understanding of their country's current status, are embedded in their national identity, and drive their collective ambitions for China's resurrection in status and reconstitution in territory.[26] Xi Jinping Thought thus invokes China's dynastic history and Confucianism and connects both to today's pursuit of the Chinese Dream: domestic prosperity and harmony that beget international influence and stature.

In practice, these sensibilities are reflected in the CCP's vehemence in combating anything that might have even the appearance of meddling in China's internal affairs or threatening its territorial integrity. This includes modernization of the PLA and foreign policies that are aggressive about maritime claims, that are reactive to perceived diplomatic slights, and that exercise the PRC's economic power to combat what it views as international efforts to support the government of Taiwan. Internally, the CCP is exerting Party control over almost all elements of the sociopolitical life of Chinese citizens, measures designed to defend the CCP's ideological program from any outside contamination that might incite fragmentation and unrest. Some of these behaviors challenge U.S. interests and some of them are offensive to liberal principles, but this does not make them an assault on the post–war order.

Free Trade

In 2021, China introduced a new phase in its foreign policy agenda through the presentation and implementation of three global initiatives, one each for development, security, and civilization. These initiatives curated concepts and themes that have long been features of China's government documents and official speeches, and they explain past and ongoing activities at the same time that they presage new ones.

None of these initiatives, however, is suggestive of a broad reshaping of China's approach to international trade. All indications are that it remains committed to globalization, which Xi Jinping in 2022 called "an unstoppable historical trend . . . that will boost the free flow of capital and technology, unleash the full potential of innovation and creativity, and foster synergy in boosting global economic growth". All countries should therefore "uphold the WTO-centered multilateral trading system, remove barriers to trade, investment and technology, and keep the global economy open" to ensure "that all countries enjoy equal rights, follow the rules as equals, and share equal opportunities".[27]

China of course did respond to President Trump's imposition of tariffs in 2018 in kind, placing its own set of barriers on U.S. agricultural products and other goods.[28] It by comparison took relatively measured retaliatory steps in the aftermath of the Biden administration's October 2022 imposition of export controls and subsequent limitations on U.S. investment in China's high technology sector. In July 2023 Beijing began restricting the export of metals classified by the United States as "critical to U.S. economic and national security" because they are integral to the production of semiconductors, electric vehicles, solar cells, fiber-optic cables, and other electronic components.[29]

China otherwise has maintained its commitment to its regional and other free trade agreements and is experimenting with new internal mechanisms to expand the terms of free trade even further, through measures like eliminating customs controls and other government restrictions in select cities.[30] It also has taken measures to address two substantial irritants in the U.S.-China trade relationship. In 2020, it revised its foreign investment controls to include market-liberalizing principles—for example, giving foreign investment the same standing as native investment, and establishing new protections for intellectual property. This same law creates new market openness by increasing the number of industries in which foreign investment is now welcome and decreasing those in which it is not.[31]

China's participation in international finance and in its post-war institutions also has been durable. China today holds major shares in the IMF and the World Bank and is the largest provider of infrastructure development finance in the world and the largest bilateral creditor to low and middle income countries.[32] Its relationship with the IMF has been characterized by a leading expert as "a close partnership" and its relationship with the World Bank as "long and positive".[33]

Although its own loan practices, exercised primarily through the China Development Bank (CDB), the China Eximbank, and the China International Development Cooperation Agency (CIDCA), have been described by U.S. and other western commentators and politicians as unfair and predatory, these accusations often are made without context, and there is evidence suggesting that they are overblown.[34] Consistent with its overall approach to BRI as part of its larger globalization strategy, experts describe the practices of these Chinese lenders as being more similar to those of the commercial sector than to those of liberal governments: they are done largely on a bilateral basis, require repayment on shorter timelines, and are at higher interest rates. China also has been unlikely to cancel or forgive debt—with the exception of the small percentage of loans provided as intentionally zero-interest foreign aid loans—although it has been willing to reschedule to extend the repayment period.[35]

Experts on the history of Chinese infrastructure finance abroad have objected to depictions of these differences as evidence of intentional exploitation and have closely examined a number of the most famously cited instances of "debt-trap diplomacy". In the case of Sri Lanka's Hambantota port, for example, which often is used as an exemplar of China's attempts to take advantage of debtor nations, researchers presented findings that Chinese banks "have never actually seized an asset from any country, much less the port of Hambantota". More broadly, they describe China's approach as a creditor to developing countries overseas as "probing and experimental, a learning process marked by frequent adjustments" and note that they are changing their strategy to better identify and handle risk—political and economic.[36]

China's creditor relationships are now supplemented by the Global Development Initiative (GDI), which does not replace but accompanies and frames the Belt and Road Initiative (BRI). Whereas BRI is part of China's approach to opening its economy and engaging new markets, GDI is explicitly development-focused; there is no expectation of economic return to China. Xi Jinping introduced GDI in a speech to the U.N. General Assembly in 2021, presenting it in part as a response to the shared international failure to improve the health and well-being of the world's populations by meeting the U.N.'s own sustainable development goals (SDGs). To redress this failure, the GDI proposes to be a framework for galvanizing and coordinating multilateral funds to support "small and beautiful" or "small and smart" projects designed not to move a state's macro-economic indicators but rather to enhance the lived experiences of its people. These behaviors are what would be expected of a state that wishes to retain the post-war financial institutions, not one that wishes to undermine them.[37]

Multilateralism

Two of China's new initiatives, the Global Security Initiative (GSI) and the Global Civilization Initiative (GCI), are oriented around China's concepts for multilateralism. The GSI distills decades of China's security pronouncements and activities into a statement of worldview and constituent principles.[38] Here, emphasis is on the reduction of state insecurity—the "root cause" of war—to be achieved through reaffirmation of the U.N. Charter's rejection of the use of force in international relations, through the use of the U.N. and of other multilateral institutions for dialogue, consultation, and conflict resolution, and by the responsible, non-hegemonic exercise of power by "major countries", most especially as regards their stewardship of nuclear weapons.[39] China has presented its engagement in the Middle East, most especially the 2023 normalization of relations between Iran and Saudi Arabia, as a demonstration of the success of the GSI's process (its coordination of "security concepts") and of its ability to produce policy outcomes (its "convergence of interests").[40]

The Global Civilization Initiative is more philosophical, presenting Xi Jinping's understanding of the "common values of humanity" as "peace, development, equity, justice, democracy, and freedom" and defining what they require of states.[41] Its central premise is that the common values of humanity can only be achieved through modernization, and so it is the obligation of governments to pursue policies that generate "not only material abundance but also cultural-ethical enrichment" for their people.[42] This requires an opening up of a state's sources of economic productivity; non-judgmental and non-extractive investments in others' economies; maintenance of, attention to, and mutual curiosity about a people's history, its "civilization", or what in the West might be called cultural identity; and mutual tolerance, indeed protection, of civilizational diversity.

These themes, again, are not new in Chinese narratives. Their curation into the GCI, however, suggests that China now is seeking to create a conceptual framework that is understandable and appealing to others. The ideal formulation, for China, would allow it to promote such activities as people-to-people exchanges while also strictly defining sovereignty such that liberal efforts to promote individual human rights and democracy are understood to constitute a form of interference in another's internal affairs and, therefore, are precluded by the U.N. Charter.

Even putting aside disagreement about the definitions of such foundational terms as democracy, equity, justice, and freedom, China's international behavior is not a study in purity. Its response to Russia's invasion of Ukraine in 2022 was not to mount a rousing defense of the U.N. Charter or of sovereignty but rather was a weak and unconvincing attempt at principled neutrality. It has since neither overtly broken the West's sanctions regime nor been scrupulous in adhering to it and has worked ardently to distinguish what has happened in Ukraine, and why, from what might happen in Taiwan, and why.[43] And although it insists that globalization "is the trend of the times" and that states "should open up, not close down . . . and uphold the multilateral trading system with the World Trade Organization at its center", it has levied non-WTO-compliant formal sanctions and informal embargoes on states and other entities. In 2019, for example, Chinese television famously stopped televising NBA basketball games to communicate its displeasure that an executive with the Houston Rockets had expressed support for pro-democracy demonstrators in Hong Kong.[44] In this instance and in others, China has been punitive in response to actions that, in Beijing's view, challenge a core PRC interest. This is especially true of its reactions to behaviors it contends violate PRC sovereignty, for example, by furthering Taiwan's international autonomy or supporting democracy in Hong Kong.[45]

So too, despite its insistence that resolutions to intractable conflicts of interest are to be sought through U.N. and other institutional mechanisms, and regardless of its protestations against threats and intimidation, the PRC has a long and still-growing record of using overtly threatening and intimidating military maneuvers to pursue unresolved territorial and resource claims. Along its contested border with India the PRC has been recurrently provocative—for example, by creating troop encampments in 2013 and breaking ground on a road construction project in a disputed area in 2017—exacerbating tensions that in 2020 and 2021 led to violent and even deadly exchanges between the two states' militaries.

In its near seas, China is not unique but is particularly active in using non-traditional and novel tactics to solidify its position. China is not the only member of the neighborhood to create artificial landmasses and to emplace buildings, runways, military equipment, and people on them to solidify maritime claims, though it has far exceeded others in the extent of the effort, having built 3,200 new acres of land compared, for example, to Vietnam's 420.[46] So too has the PRC been the most frequent but not an always-present member of dyads engaged in militarized jostling over claims to islands, atolls, and undersea resources. Japan and Taiwan have had tense exchanges in disputed waters, as have Vietnam and Indonesia, Vietnam and the Philippines, Vietnam and Thailand, Vietnam and Taiwan, the Philippines and Taiwan, the Philippines and Malaysia, with a number of these instances including harm to ships and their crews.[47] Still, these behaviors and, certainly, China's constant campaign of diplomatic, economic, information, and military pressure on the people of Taiwan, designed to persuade them to concede to unification with the mainland, are patently contrary to its narrative commitment to non-threatening and non-intimidating modes of conflict resolution. So too are they in contravention of the U.N. Convention on the Law of the Sea (UNCLOS), to which China is a signatory.

It is important, however, that in explaining these behaviors, China consistently seeks recourse in international rules, and often with some basis. Many of the region's overlapping territorial claims have to do with historic titles and rights, which do have standing in international rule-making bodies.[48] China has largely—though not wholly—sought to address differences in interpretation of these histories through UNCLOS and through other mechanisms, for example, the 2002 Association of Southeast Asian Nations (ASEAN)-China Declaration on the Conduct of Parties in the South China Sea. In the widely cited instance of its refusal to comply with the results of the 2016 South China Sea Arbitral Tribunal, for example, China's objections were founded in its interpretation of the Tribunal's jurisdiction—an interpretation it elaborated at great length and that the Tribunal took, and treated, seriously.[49]

While these ongoing legal machinations have yet to produce any resolution, China's combination of de facto action with protests against and rejections of some de jure processes and outcomes is far preferable to the outright use of force. It also suggests that China does not object to having rules or that it rejects the perception that rules are embodied not in bombs and rockets but in treaties and institutions.

Two Ideas and Four Institutions

The United States and China have participated in the institutions of the post–World War II international order, have followed their rules and have broken them, and have sometimes levied consequences and sometimes haven't. Both states also profess ongoing attachment to the principle of territorial integrity, a commitment to sustainable development, and a desire to maintain a global economy that runs on rules that facilitate the worldwide movement of goods, money, ideas, and people.

U.S. officials nonetheless regularly assert that the post-war rules-based order is today under a new and serious kind of strain, that it is at risk of being degraded and possibly entirely deconstructed by states that are dissatisfied with it, China primary among them. China thus is categorized as a revisionist working in league with others—most notably but not exclusively Russia—to undermine the United States and the post–war order.

China does use diplomatic dissembling, economic and military coercion, and selective interpretations of history to pursue its interests, but what China has said, and done, over time and into the present day suggest that China is more in support of than opposed to the post–war order's two ideas and four institutions. It has made sometimes demanding domestic economic adjustments to gain entry into trade regimes and continues to promote globalization in rhetoric and in policy. Although it has grown its military in size and invested in improving its performance, it is not ideologically or territorially expansionist, its nuclear arsenal has for decades been underweight as compared to its overall national power, and the use of force has not been a primary feature of its foreign policy.[50] It lobbied to gain entry into the post-war institutions, has worked effectively within them, and has sought to redress its dissatisfactions and forward its interests by agitating for changes to their rules.

The project for U.S. foreign policy for now thus is not to contain, convert, or befriend China. It also is not to try to resolve fundamental differences by achieving a shared understanding of individual rights or of the content and limitations of state sovereignty; attempting to do so is more likely to aggravate areas of divergence than it is to generate opportunities for progress. The work instead is to capitalize on China's attachment to the current order and to reinvigorate America's own. This has not been the direction of travel for U.S. foreign policy since the election of Donald Trump in 2016, but the track is not yet so rigidly laid that it is too late to correct course.

The United States can begin to do so by rebalancing the distribution of attention it gives to the post–war order's military backbone relative to the order's economic and diplomatic machinery. Ongoing modernization of the PLA, which serves to deter a U.S. use of force, does require China's regional neighbors, and the United States, to continue to invest in their own militaries to deter China in return. Aggressive expansion of U.S. warfighting capability and associated activity in the Indo-Pacific, however, is unnecessary to achieve U.S. regional objectives and runs the risk of crossing the "culminating point of deterrence": the threshold at which efforts to deter become less likely to produce restraint than they are to incite reaction.[51]

The emphasis in U.S. national security strategy on ensuring its warfighting advantage over China also is crowding out engagement on other of the region's non-military priorities, like addressing transnational crime, illicit resource extraction, climate change, climate-caused security threats, and economic development. If this reflects a mistaken assumption that local governments are more fearful of China's military than they are interested in addressing these concerns, then continuing to under-treat them will be counterproductive to the U.S. goal of retaining regional influence.

If the strategic objective, moreover, is to maintain a structure and character of international order that privileges U.S. interests and preferences, then the United States will need to seek to include the maximum possible substance it desires in the rules that the post-war institutions produce. This is not a bromide about the ability of institutions to constrain powerful states or about the power of diplomatic engagement to "settle scores" and "mend ties".[52] Neither is it for purposes of pleasing allies and partners or for reputational rehabilitation. China has made significant investments of capital and talent in expanding and enhancing its ability to shape the operations and outputs of the post-war institutions, with the goal of advancing its interests and values. If the United States prefers that these institutions remain central to the post–war order, and if it prefers that the rules they produce hew more toward U.S. interests and values than toward China's, then it will need to work actively and effectively within them to make it so.

National Prosperity

The motivations that produced the GATT, the WTO, the IMF, and World Bank were the beliefs that trade generates national prosperity and that free trade reduces the likelihood that interstate disputes about trade will cause war. The Biden administration's international economic policy suggests that it believed otherwise—that the free movement of finance, goods, services, and people across borders has instead been harmful to the United States, reducing the availability of gainful employment, creating dangerous dependencies, and unfairly advantaging China. It therefore imposed barriers to trade for purposes of growing domestic industries that it defined as having strategic importance—those central to economic productivity and military capability in the future—that produce jobs, that create supply chain resilience, and that do so in ways that minimize China's role in them.

Continuing to move U.S. policy away from the tenets of globalization will produce one of two outcomes. The first is that it will achieve what the Biden administration wished it to achieve, boosting domestic productivity, catalyzing innovation, reducing vulnerability to China, and limiting China's ability to develop the industries of the future, all without causing serious disruption to the operation of the overall global economy. This will require other governments to be convinced that what is good and bad for the U.S. economy is good and bad for their economies too. And it will require them therefore to be willing to enter into agreements focused not on reducing barriers to trade but on striking a careful balance of conditions that make trade not free, but still beneficial enough. The other possible outcome is that it won't work—that striking this careful balance is too difficult to achieve, and so long-time

U.S. trading partners, friends, and even defense allies will become less inclined to have economic relationships with the United States and more inclined to pursue them with others, including with China.

The alternative to placing this bet, of course, is to recommit to free trade, including to the WTO as the primary forum for establishing terms of trade and reconciling disputes. This approach would entail working actively to address dissatisfactions among members about the current distribution of benefits and responsibilities and investing in improving the organization's ability to monitor and enforce the rules it produces. This will mean making procedural and substantive compromises, but if managed skillfully these are likely preferable to a circumstance in which the cost of goods and services for U.S. citizens increases while the overall ability of the United States to influence the global economy decreases. This is especially true in the digital domain, where rules and regulations about the flow of data and of data services are nascent and their implications for the international economy are significant.

The U.S. approach to engagement in global development can also benefit from a considerable conceptual and practical reorientation. There is a need to make investments in developing nations a more prominent element of U.S. foreign policy and one that is far more responsive to their expressed needs. As explained by the former Secretary General of the Pacific Islands Forum:

> While we hear of a range of new economic, development, and environmental programs and policies that exclude China, we experience the primary geostrategic focus as defense. . . . At the regional level, rather than seeking to surpass China's improved position by also delivering on our development agenda, the response from the United States and its allies has been to subsume our narrative under their own geostrategic framework . . . [the U.S.] Indo-Pacific strategy is incompatible with Blue Pacific priorities and values. . . . It is a traditional, defense-centric understanding of security that sits in stark contrast to our broader definition that recognizes the expanded concept of security that includes human security, economic security, humanitarian assistance, environmental security, cybersecurity, and transnational crime, as well as regional cooperation to build resilience to disasters and climate change.[53]

U.S. unwillingness to reform the IMF to give China and other developing countries significantly more say in to whom and how loans are offered, moreover, and its resistance to supporting a 2023 allocation of emergency funds given the "combined external debt, food, climate, and other crises contributing to one of the worst global economic situations in decades" are unhelpful.[54] And while U.S. announcements of intent to reinvigorate action on the U.N. Sustainable Development Goals (SDG) to "reshape and scale up the World Bank" and to "deliver game-changing projects to close the infrastructure gap in developing countries" through the Partnership for Global Infrastructure and Investment are useful, implementation is necessary.[55] In short, the United States has been underperforming in listening to and addressing the needs of the developing world, and if it wishes to compete for influence—which is, to say, to convince those populations that China's development model is less beneficial than that of the United States—then it will need to better make that case through action.

Great Power Peace

The post–war order's economic structure is to a large degree a reflection of its most core conviction and earnestly-felt hope: that there should not be—indeed, that with the advent of nuclear weapons there cannot be—another great power war. This is the order's center of gravity, and it is this feature that U.S. strategy must be most focused on preserving into the future. Doing so will require that the United States attend, but not overreact, to the fact that China's military power has and will continue to grow and to change regional dynamics, sometimes in ways that challenge U.S. interests.

The United States has defense obligations to longstanding treaty allies and an abiding interest in stability throughout the Indo-Pacific. These commitments are not fungible—the United States is not leaving the region—and they must be managed in such a way that they demonstrate to China the limits of tolerable behavior while also being attuned to China's own demonstrations of the same. Some of this can and will be communicated diplomatically, but the reality of current U.S.-China relations means that much of it also will be communicated through mutual military signaling.

This most immediately and dangerously is the case regarding the Taiwan question, but China's military capabilities and willingness now to use them more liberally in its surrounding seas make it increasingly applicable to other of the region's contested sovereignty claims as well. The United States can best respond to these new conditions by reinforcing its heretofore steady and patient strategy for contributing to regional peace and stability: by making clear that its interest is in the processes through which these disputes are resolved, not in the substance of their outcomes, and by using its diplomatic, economic, and military tools of influence to encourage dialogue and to discourage dangerous behavior.

The Special Case of Taiwan

Since 1979, the U.S. national interest in the status of Taiwan has been that Taipei and Beijing resolve their dispute peacefully. It has sought to maintain the conditions necessary for the two parties to do so by implementing a strategy of dual deterrence: the United States provides neither an unconditional commitment to Taipei that it will come to its defense militarily, which deters it from declaring independence, nor an unconditional commitment to Beijing that it will not, which deters it from using force to achieve unification.

Over the course of 40 years, ensuring the credibility of dual-deterrence and thereby keeping the path to peaceful resolution open has been achieved through the adoption of a constellation of nuanced official positions: the First (1972), Second (1979), and Third (1982) Communiques; the Taiwan Relations Act (TRA); and the Six Assurances (1982). Together, these positions are known as the "One-China Policy". It is a policy that does two equally important things. First, it acknowledges but does not accept or agree with the PRC's view that there is one China, and that Taiwan is part of China. Second, it establishes the U.S. intent to continue to engage in unofficial relations with the island's government and its people.

This strategy of dual deterrence has at times required active reaffirmation. There have been instances in which China's cross-Strait behavior has been provocative, and so the specter of U.S. force was transitioned into corporeal shows of U.S. force—the dispatch of the *Independence* carrier strike group in 1996 in response to a series of military activities opposite Taiwan in advance of its upcoming election, for example. These events, however, have been transitory, and until recently, the United States largely has been cautious about giving even the appearance of breaking faith with the One-China Policy.

As China's military capability has grown, however, many in the United States have become restive about U.S. policy and posture, concerned that it no longer is adequate to deter Beijing from moving forcibly against Taiwan. Some have made the case that such an outcome would degrade the global reputation and regional power of the United States and that its long-term effect would be to encourage Chinese aggression elsewhere, inevitably leading to war with the United States.[56] Many who take this view find remedy in substantially reinforcing U.S. and allied regional military capability.

Whether one agrees or disagrees that a use of force against Taiwan is the first step in Chinese pursuit of regional hegemony on its way to a bid for global primacy, such an act would unquestionably be a disaster for the people of Taiwan, would do immediate and serious economic harm to the United States—indeed to the world—and would be a severe breach of the post–war order's foundational principle of non-aggression. The U.S. interest therefore remains supporting peace and stability in the Taiwan Strait, and an effective strategy will pursue that interest without unduly increasing the risk of war.

Such a strategy must be premised on the twin facts that the United States no longer can be confident that it would decisively defeat every type of PLA use of force in the Taiwan Strait and that it is unlikely to regain that kind of superiority any time soon, if ever.[57] Neither, however, can China be confident that it would win in any given contingency if the United States were to choose to engage. To the contrary, authoritative analysis has concluded that it simply is not possible to predict who would win such a war, only to calculate how much everyone stands to lose.[58] There is, therefore, no need for the United States to send massive infusions of warfighting capability into East Asia. Such an approach would be prohibitively expensive, provocative, and, given China's natural advantage of proximity and its ability to design and equip a strategy accordingly, unlikely to succeed.

It will instead be sufficient, and much more fiscally and geopolitically responsible, for the U.S. military posture to evolve organically with the pace of change in technology. For the United States, this will mean hardening the information systems—the command and control networks—upon which its military depends. It also requires developing the concepts and acquiring the tools and platforms needed to operate in the harsh conditions and large expanses of the Western Pacific's maritime environment. The Biden administration's pursuit of small access points distributed throughout the Western Pacific is a sensible element of such a strategy and one that has the virtue of being useful beyond the special case of Taiwan. So too has the U.S. Marine Corps made admirable strides in configuring itself to operate cohesively over time and distance—to campaign—in the Western Pacific. It has released and made progress on a series of strategy designs that describe a force that is mobile, equipped with modern sensing and information technologies, and positioned to respond rapidly to indications and warnings of an adversarial action. U.S. efforts to work with Taiwan on using advances in military technology to increase the difficulty and cost of attacking the island, through direct defense and through all-of-society preparedness, are equally well founded.

Maintaining peace and stability over the Taiwan Strait, however, will require more than managing military dynamics. In the first instance, a strategy that clearly signals to Beijing that the use of force would have not only direct and significant military costs as a result of Taiwanese preparedness and, possibly, from U.S. intervention, but also severe political and economic consequences is more prudent than one that relies on military deterrence alone.[59] Toward this end, the international community usefully can engage with Taiwan in ways that increase the perception that other countries would be more likely than not to participate in diplomatic and economic retribution for any unprovoked Chinese use of force against the island. The United States must also continue to demonstrate its commitment to deterring Taiwan from declaring independence, again in service of a mutually and peacefully achieved resolution to the two parties' dispute about the island's status. It is here that U.S. activity was relatively undisciplined under the Biden administration, despite its insistence that the United States remains committed to the One-China Policy.

After assuming office in January 2020, the Biden administration was increasingly overt in its diplomacy with Taiwan. In 2021, it for the first time extended an invitation to the island's de facto ambassador to attend the presidential inauguration, revised State Department guidance to widen the scope of acceptable interactions between the U.S. diplomatic corps and their Taiwanese counterparts, and included Taiwan in the Summit for Democracy.[60] Far from decreasing arms sales over time as agreed in the 3rd Communique, the United States has used the TRA and 1982 Six Assurances—statements of U.S. intent to retain latitude in arms sales to Taiwan—to justify increasing it.[61] It has not only acknowledged the presence of a modest number of U.S. troops on the island but has added to their number.[62] All of this has been accompanied by the calls of former and current U.S. government officials for the United States to abandon the strategy of dual deterrence and in other ways to clearly communicate U.S. solidarity with Taiwan.[63]

China's policies also have contributed to increased tension in the Strait's three-way dynamic. Xi Jinping has been strident in expressing his commitment to unification and the PRC has intensified its use of economic, political, and digital coercion of the Taiwan people. So too has it reacted harshly to what Beijing interprets as indicators that the United States and Taiwan are seeking to change the status quo by further degrading the One-China Policy and moving the island toward independence. This is a longstanding but intensifying pattern, visible in its 1996 missile test timed to coincide with an election featuring (and ultimately electing) pro-independence candidate Lee Teng-hui; in circumnavigational flights around Taiwan in 2019 that followed reports of the Trump administration's intention to sell Taipei F-16 fighters; in combat exercises in 2020 that crossed the median line in the Taiwan Strait, coincident with the visit to Taipei of a senior U.S. official; in the attention-getting ADIZ incursions in October 2021, after which China's Foreign Ministry highlighted Beijing's objections to U.S. arms sales to Taiwan and the transiting of U.S. military vessels through the Taiwan Strait; in January 2022, when 39 Chinese jets flew toward the island after the United States announced the transit of two carrier strike groups through the South China Sea; and especially in its large and prolonged military exercises around Taiwan in the aftermath of then-speaker of the House Nancy Pelosi's visit in August 2022.[64]

The interactions between the U.S. intent to deter Beijing from a use of force and Beijing's intent to deter Taiwan from declaring independence and, ultimately, to achieve unification are increasingly dangerous. Even if none of the three participants crosses another's threshold intentionally, it may do so by accident, with terrible consequences. The United States cannot control all of these dynamics, but it can and should remain attentive to the fact that there is no way to know what that tipping point will be for Xi Jinping and consider its actions carefully for their alignment with the One-China Policy.

Beyond Taiwan

While most analysts and scholars of China acknowledge that Beijing has become aggressive in asserting its interpretation of the geographic boundaries of its sovereignty and of what it presents as its historic rights—inclusive of Taiwan, Tibet, and in various regions along its border with India—few consider it to be territorially expansionist. Although they currently attract considerable attention, China's claims to the islands and rocks in the South China Sea are long-standing, dating, according to one scholar, to "well before the establishment of the PRC".[65] The now-infamous nine-dash line similarly is not new but rather has its origins in the drawings of private cartographers working in the 1930s. In the 1940s, the Chinese government regained islands occupied by Japan during World War II and, after conducting "further inspections and surveys . . . internally circulated an atlas . . . drawing an eleven-dash line to indicate the geographical scope of its authority over the South China Sea".[66] Two of the dashes were excised in the early 1950s after negotiation with Vietnam, and the count has remained at nine over the decades since.[67] Although it is insistent that it retains rights in the maritime space the line denotes, China has not fully specified the nature or extent of these claims but "has been continually exploring the legal framing" of them since the 1990s, "in line with the development of international maritime law".[68]

Whatever the basis of China's position, its claims and its increasingly hostile activities to forward them are a source of considerable friction regionally and in its relations with the United States. The U.S. objectives in the waters of East Asia and of the more broadly conceived Indo-Pacific have been articulated as ensuring that "problems will be dealt with openly; rules will be reached transparently and applied fairly; and goods, ideas, and people will flow freely across land, the seas, the skies, and cyberspace".[69] The goal, in other words, is for disputes to be resolved peacefully and in a manner that does not disrupt the operation of the global economy. U.S. strategy thus should be designed to make dialogue and agreement more available and appealing, and obfuscation, closure, and aggression more difficult to achieve and less likely to work.[70] This will require the United States and its allies and partners to define which behaviors constitute deviation from standards, expectations, and norms that exceed acceptable limits. They also will need to commit adequate economic, diplomatic, and military capital to exercise vigilance and consistency in recognizing and responding quickly when China exceeds those limits.

Given the physical realities of geography and the challenges it presents for the U.S. military, communicating to China the unprofitability of aggression will require regional actors to be more demonstrably prepared to defend their territorial and access interests with their own conventional military capability. They should be encouraged to do so, however, through the development of operational concepts and the acquisition of assets and platforms most suited to homeland and coastal defense, not to expeditionary warfare. While the line between the two can be blurry, it is possible for states to purchase, posture, and communicate in ways that provide a preponderance of evidence in one direction or the other. It also is necessary for U.S. allies and partners throughout the Indo-Pacific to have shared expectations in the event of crisis. This will require close consultation to ensure alignment on the risks associated with particular forms of independent and coordinated action, to ensure mutual understanding of risk tolerance, and to establish the boundaries and constraints on cooperative military activity in the event the United States responds to a contingency.

The United States and regional partners can also reduce the likelihood of inadvertent conflict by using means other than the transit of military vessels to reinforce their insistence on unimpeded access to common air and sea lanes, and to make violations of established fishing, resource,

and transit rights more difficult to achieve. The use of new and afford-
able technologies, available today, can extend the reach and duration of
surveillance and intelligence collection that can provide better visibility
and timeliness in recognizing indications and warnings of potentially
threatening or illicit activities.[71] These capabilities can be used by the
United States and other regional actors to recognize and respond rapidly
to such behaviors. Even if this tightening of the operating environment
doesn't incentivize negotiation, it can prevent de facto changes and preserve the status quo.

In the near term, the United States Navy is the service most available to conduct response operations. The U.S. Coast Guard (USCG) is
well suited to the task, but it is small and, housed in the Department of
Homeland Security, its mission is U.S. coastal defense. Investment in
USCG and other programs that equip and train regional coast guards,
however, are an efficient means through which to shift work away from
the U.S. military and to local forces. Doing so not only will give regional
governments more control over their own security environments but
also will decrease the likelihood of an unwanted U.S. military interaction with the PLA—a risk, in the interim, that the United States will need
to continue to manage carefully. China, it bears noting, has a non-trivial
record of addressing territorial disputes either through settlement or
through delay.[72] The former may be preferable to the latter, but the latter is far preferable to war, and so the United States should be equally
inclined toward patience where disputes are especially intractable.

There also has been much heat but little light, regarding China's
ambitions for creating a network of overseas basing and access arrangements. There is much that remains uncertain and unknown about China's motivations for pursuing military-capable outposts overseas, much
less about its intentions for putting them to use. This largely reflects the
reality that there is more than one plausible alternative explanation for
these activities and the fact that there is more than one plausible use that
can be made of them. The 2023 U.S. Department of Defense "Report on
the Military and Security Developments Involving the People's Republic
of China" captures this reality concisely:

> Official PRC sources assert that military logistics facilities, to include
> its Djibouti base, will be used to provide international public goods
> like [humanitarian assistance and disaster relief], and secure China's
> lines of communication, citizens, and assets abroad. Regardless, a
> global PLA military logistics network could disrupt U.S. military
> operations as the PRC's global military objectives evolve.[73]

Even if China's recent security agreements and those elsewhere that the DoD describes Beijing to be "very likely considering and planning for" do reflect an ambition to deploy forces overseas for a sustained period of time, for purposes of disrupting U.S. operations or otherwise, the near- and medium-term risks to the United States are low.[74] The U.S. basing advantage already resident in its established overseas infrastructure, in its demonstrated skill in managing complex host-nation relationships, and in its experience executing regional military operations is clear and durable.

The United States now has made significant, long-term diplomatic, economic, and military investments in a foreign policy agenda that treats China as an ideological and geopolitical threat. It should not therefore be surprising that its efforts to engage Beijing in issue-specific cooperation have achieved little success. In response to what the DoD describes as a "sharp increase in coercive and risky operational behavior in the East and South China seas", for example, the clear U.S. interest in establishing regular, meaningful high-level military-to-military exchanges has been met with a tepid response from China.[75] The U.S. rationale is that regular non-crisis interactions are the best way to prevent a crisis interaction from mushrooming into an unintended war. The Chinese rationale is that U.S. caution, and preferably regional retrenchment, is the best way to achieve that same goal. The United States similarly has expressed its interest in engaging with China on other issues of mutual concern, most notably climate change. Here again, China has been substantially unmoved.

The United States will need to accept that it is unlikely to persuade Beijing to negotiate, compromise, or cooperate in the ways and places Washington would like at the same time that it makes Taiwan a central feature of its defense strategy, seeks to reinforce the U.S. military position in the Indo-Pacific, and implements cultural, diplomatic, and economic policies that constrain China's role in the international community and global economy. Given their importance, the United States should continue to press these cases, though with the understanding that doing so is in service of laying groundwork for more fruitful exchanges if and when conditions are more favorable, and without the expectation of immediate returns. The exception, and an area in which the United States might find more purchase, is an issue of undeniable bilateral security concern: forging agreement on abstaining from AI-enabled cyber intrusions into the two nations' respective nuclear enterprises. Beijing might be willing to address this subject regardless of the overall state of the U.S.-China relationship, given its worry about the vulnerability of its second-strike capability and given the potentially existential consequences of such an operation gone wrong. This will not itself set the course for U.S.-China relations, but it could, at a minimum, allow these states to demonstrate to each other and to the world their desire to avert one worst-case scenario and might, at a maximum, over time create an inroad to productive dialogues in other domains as well.

An Imperfect Order

The United States and China have now arrived at a point in their respective development that the ways in which their national identities and their ambitions overlap, clash, and interact will set the terms of life not just for themselves or for each other but for humanity. Both therefore have the responsibility to discover how to manage their relationship in ways that better the human condition and how to avoid those that worsen it. Superficial characterizations and false binaries impede engagement and, in so doing, not only are unhelpful but, increasingly, also are dangerous. The goal of U.S. policy must instead be to infuse the U.S.-China relationship with as much stability as possible—by increasing the capability of U.S. allies and partners to defend their interests and detect and respond quickly when China subverts extant norms and standards, by reminding China that the U.S. regional military presence is there to support peaceful resolution of disagreements, and by pragmatically engaging China within the institutional structures of the post–war order.

The United States cannot itself determine the nature, tenor, or direction of its relationship with China. But Washington should not overlook or be dismissive of the extent to which its approach to Beijing can influence Beijing's approach to it. It is unrealistic to believe that China will make concessions about its core interests or that it will consistently choose to pursue those interests in ways that conform with the standards and norms preferred by the United States. But converting China is not the goal. The goal is to disincentivize China from resolving its disputes through the use of force and to provide it adequate peaceful—if sometimes coercive—pathways through which to pursue its interests.

Even those who take the view that China's ambitions are expansive and malign acknowledge that Beijing is highly attentive to the United States—to its economic performance, to its military capability, to its overseas activities, and to the health of its internal politics. There is ample evidence that the United States is a central feature in Beijing's evaluation of its external environment and that it quite often calibrates its own policies in response to what it sees emanating from Washington D.C. This is especially true regarding Taiwan, where Beijing makes it known that it is paying excruciating attention to every minute detail of U.S. rhetoric and action, and it similarly is present in China's counters to U.S. economic policies. Were it otherwise, there would be no trade war, and neither would there be concerns about retribution for U.S. export controls, outbound investment restrictions, and economic de-risking.[76]

The United States, in short, has ample means—including the post-war infrastructure, robust relationships with allies and partners, and America's own considerable strengths—through which it has and can continue to influence China's behavior.[77] The work of strategic competition is to determine how to do so effectively and safely. It is worrisome that the U.S. national security community seems ever less inclined to find ways to do so and ever more inclined instead toward categorical narratives and combative policies. This is despite the fact that the United States is as physically secure today as any state ever has been, at any time in recorded history. Its and others' nuclear arsenals mean not only that the likelihood of an attack on the United States by another country is exceptionally low but also that the stakes of great power war are not the survival of America or of Americans but the survival of everyone, everywhere.

The likelihood of global calamity therefore varies with the purposefulness with which the United States and China seek to avoid it. This will require a discipline in trying not to provoke each other's fears; a readiness to acknowledge areas of agreement where they exist; a commitment to finding opportunities to reconcile differences whenever possible; and the exercise of great skill in minimizing the consequences of those differences where necessary. It will not be enough to identify discrete areas where cooperation might be possible. Everything will instead depend upon whether these two nations succeed in forging structures and habits of international political life that sustain a mutually tolerable, if mutually imperfect, order.

* * *

Notes

1 "United States National Security Strategy" (Washington, DC: The White House), October 2022.
2 Xi Jinping, "Light Up Our Way Forward with Multilateralism", Special address at the World Economic Forum Virtual Event of the Davos Agenda, January 25, 2021; Xi Jinping, "Create a Better Post-Covid World", Speech at a virtual session of the 2022 World Economic Forum, January 17, 2022; Xi Jinping, "Maintain World Peace and Stability", keynote speech at the opening ceremony of the Boao Forum for Asia Annual Conference, April 21, 2022.

3 Steve Holland and Alexandra Alper, "'America Is Back' – Biden Touts Muscular Foreign Policy in First Diplomatic Speech", *Reuters*, February 4, 2021, www.reuters.com/article/idUSKBN2A507W/; Monica Duffy Toft and Sidita Kushi, *Dying by the Sword: The Militarization of US Foreign Policy* (New York: Oxford Academic), 2023.

4 "United States National Security Strategy", p. 8; "Remarks by President Biden Before the 76th Session of the United Nations General Assembly" (Washington, DC: The White House), September 21, 2021, www.whitehouse.gov/briefing-room/speeches-remarks/2021/09/21/remarks-by-president-biden-before-the-76th-session-of-the-united-nations-general-assembly/.

5 Franklin Foer, *The Last Politician: Inside Joe Biden's White House and the Struggle for America's Future* (New York: Penguin Press), 2023, pp. 18–19.

6 Asma Khalid, "Biden Kept Trump's Tariffs on Chinese Imports. This Is Who Pays the Price", *NPR*, June 27, 2023, www.npr.org/2023/06/27/1184027892/china-tariffs-biden-trump.

7 Outbound investment in entities exploring quantum technology and microelectronics are also disallowed. For a good overview see: Noah Berman, "President Biden Has Banned Some U.S. Investment in China. Here's What to Know" (New York: Council on Foreign Relations), August 29, 20203, www.cfr.org/in-brief/president-biden-has-banned-some-us-investment-china-heres-what-know.

8 "Remarks by National Security Advisor Jake Sullivan on Renewing American Economic Leadership at the Brookings Institution" (Washington, DC: The Brookings Institution), April 27, 2023, www.whitehouse.gov/briefing-room/speeches-remarks/2023/04/27/remarks-by-national-security-advisor-jake-sullivan-on-renewing-american-economic-leadership-at-the-brookings-institution/.

9 Andrew Grotto, "Mitigating Ally Concerns about U.S. Semiconductor Policies" (Washington, DC: The National Bureau of Asian Research), January 21, 2023, www.nbr.org/publication/mitigating-ally-concerns-about-u-s-semiconductor-policies/.

10 Gavin Bade and Doug Palmer, "Europe Moves from Anger toward Acceptance of U.S. Climate Law", *Politico*, February 8, 2023, www.politico.com/news/2023/02/08/europe-acceptes-us-climate-law-00081619.

11 "Remarks by National Security Advisor Jake Sullivan on Renewing American Economic Leadership at the Brookings Institution"; Paul Krugman, "Why America Is Getting Tough on Trade", *The New York Times*, December 12, 2022, www.nytimes.com/2022/12/12/opinion/america-trade-biden.html.

12 Rebecca Lissner and Mira Rapp-Hooper, *An Open World: How America Can Win the Contest for Twenty-First-Century Order* (New Haven, CT: Yale University Press), 2020, p. 64; Michael J. Mazarr, Timothy R. Heath, and Astrid Stuth Cevallos, "China and the International Order" (Santa Monica, CA: RAND Corporation), 2018, www.rand.org/pubs/research_reports/RR2423.html.

13 Bryce Baschuk, "US Snub of WTO Ruling Marks a 'Step Back' in Era of Free Trade", *Bloomberg*, December 12, 2022, www.bloomberg. com/news/newsletters/2022-12-12/supply-chain-latest-us-snub-of-wto-called-a-step-back-for-trade.

14 "Fact Sheet: President Biden and G7 Leaders Formally Launch the Partnership for Global Infrastructure and Investment" (Washington, DC: The White House), June 26, 2022, www.whitehouse.gov/briefing-room/statements-releases/2022/06/26/fact-sheet-president-biden-and-g7-leaders-formally-launch-the-partnership-for-global-infrastructure-and-investment/; Oyintarelado Moses and Keren Zhu, "The Belt and Road Initiative and the Partnership for Global Infrastructure and Investment: Global Infrastructure Initiatives in Comparison", Boston University, Global China Initiative, Global Development Policy Center, GCI Working Paper 026, November 2022, www.bu.edu/gdp/files/2022/11/GCI_WP_026_BPG_FIN.pdf.

15 Michael Birnbaum and Rachel Pannett, "U.S. and China Battle for Influence in Pacific Island Nations", *The Washington Post*, July 25, 2023, www.washingtonpost.com/national-security/2023/07/25/blinken-tonga-biden-china-pacific-islands/; Patricia M. Kim, "Does the China-Solomon Islands Security Pact Portend a More Interventionist Beijing?" (Washington, DC: The Brookings Institution), May 6, 2022, www.brookings.edu/articles/does-the-china-solomon-islands-security-pact-portend-a-more-interventionist-beijing/.

16 "Congressional Budget Justification, Department of State, Foreign Operations and Related Programs" (Washington, DC: U.S. Department of State), FY2024, p. ii, www.usaid.gov/sites/default/files/2023-03/FY%202024%20CBJ%20FINAL_3.9.23_0.pdf.

17 Joshua P. Meltzer, "Rewiring US Trade Policy to Address New Global Realities", *The Hill*, November 4, 2022, https://thehill.com/opinion/international/3719612-rewiring-us-trade-policy-to-address-new-global-realities/.

18 Franklin Roosevelt, quoted in Henry Kissinger, *Diplomacy* (New York: Simon & Schuster), 1994, p. 416.

19 The emphasis on a single war was a change from the preceding decades in which the Department's planning was designed to manage two regional wars simultaneously.

20 "The Pacific Deterrence Initiative: A Budgetary Overview", *Congressional Research Service*, January 9, 2023, https://sgp.fas.org/crs/natsec/IF12303.pdf; "Indo-Pacific Strategy of the United States" (Washington, DC: The White House), February 2022, www.whitehouse.gov/wp-content/uploads/2022/02/U.S.-Indo-Pacific-Strategy.pdf.

21 Sarah A. Topol, "The America that Americans Forget", *The New York Times Magazine*, July 7, 2023, www.nytimes.com/2023/07/07/magazine/guam-american-military.html; Ryo Nakamura and Satoshi Iwaka, "U.S. Plans Naval Logistics Hubs in India to Counter China", *Nikkei*, July 7, 2023, https://asia.nikkei.com/Politics/International-relations/Indo-Pacific/U.S.-plans-naval-logistics-hubs-in-India-to-counter-China.

22 Garret Martin and James Goldgeier, "NATO, China, and the Vilnius Summit", *War on the Rocks*, July 7, 2023, https://warontherocks.com/2023/07/nato-china-and-the-vilnius-summit/.

23 Elbridge Colby, "America Must Prepare for a War over Taiwan", *Foreign Affairs*, August 10, 2022, www.foreignaffairs.com/united-states/america-must-prepare-war-over-taiwan; Michael Hirsh, "The Pentagon Is Freaking Out about a Potential War with China", *Politico*, June 9, 2023, www.politico.com/news/magazine/2023/06/09/america-weapons-china-00100373.

24 Ibid.; Hans Kristensen et al., "Strategic Posture Commission Report Calls for Broad Nuclear Buildup" (Washington, DC: Federation of American Scientists), October 12, 2023, https://fas.org/publication/strategic-posture-commission-report-calls-for-broad-nuclear-buildup/.

25 "America's Strategic Posture: The Final Report of the Congressional Commission on the Strategic Posture of the United States" (Washington, DC: Institute for Defense Analyses), 2023, p. 8, https://armedservices.house.gov/sites/republicans.armedservices.house.gov/files/Strategic-Posture-Committee-Report-Final.pdf.

26 Z. Wang, *Never Forget National Humiliation: Historical Memory in Chinese Politics and Foreign Relations* (New York: Columbia University Press), 2014.

27 "President Xi Jinping Delivered a Keynote Speech at the Opening Ceremony of the BRICS Business Forum", Ministry of Foreign Affairs of the People's Republic of China, June 22, 2022.

28 Chad P. Bown, Euijin Jung, and Zhiyao (Lucy) Lu, "China's Retaliation to Trump's Tariffs" (Washington, DC: Peterson Institute for International Economics), *Trade and Investment Policy Watch*, June 22, 2018, www.piie.com/blogs/trade-and-investment-policy-watch/chinas-retaliation-trumps-tariffs.

29 Sean Stein et al., "China Slaps Export Restrictions on Two Critical Metals", *Global Policy Watch*, July 6, 2023, www.globalpolicywatch.com/2023/07/china-slaps-export-restrictions-on-two-critical-metals/.

30 Keyu Jun, *The New China Playbook: Beyond Socialism and Capitalism* (New York: Viking), 2023, pp. 227–256.

31 Xianjun Feng and Chuanhui Wang, "China's Foreign Investment Law: Moving Toward Greater Liberalization?", *Penn State Journal of Law & International Affairs*, Vol. 10, No. 2, 2022, pp. 116–195, https://elibrary.law.psu.edu/cgi/viewcontent.cgi?article=1319&context=jlia.

32 Sebastian Horn, Carmen M. Reinhart, and Christoph Trebesch, "China's Overseas Lending", *Journal of International Economics*, Vol. 133, 2021, pp. 1–32, https://doi.org/10.1016/j.jinteco.2021.103539; Suisheng Zhao, *The Dragon Roars Back: Transformational Leaders and Dynamics of Chinese Foreign Policy* (Stanford, CA: Stanford University Press), 2023.

33 David Dollar, "Reluctant Player: China's Approach to International Economic Institutions" (Washington, DC: The Brookings

Institution), September 14, 2020, www.brookings.edu/articles/reluctant-player-chinas-approach-to-international-economic-institutions/.

34 David Dollar, "Setting the Record Straight on China's Engagement in Africa" (Washington, DC: The Brookings Institution), July 11, 2016, www.brookings.edu/articles/setting-the-record-straight-on-chinas-engagement-in-africa/.

35 Kai Wang, "China: Is it Burdening Poor Countries with Unsustainable Debt?", *BBC Reality Check*, January 6, 2022, www.bbc.com/news/59585507; "China's Approach to Sovereign Lending and Debt Restructuring: A Primer for African Public Debt Managers" (South Africa: Collaborative Africa Budget Reform Initiative (CABRI)), 2021, www.cabri-sbo.org/uploads/files/Documents/China-approach-to-sovereign-lending-and-debt-restructuring-A-primer-for-African-public-debt-managers.pdf.

36 One expert describes Beijing as becoming "more parsimonious in starting new projects" and notes that the imposition of "new capital controls imposed in 2016 to stem capital flight made it harder to finance [overseas direct investment]". See: Arthur R. Kroeber, "The Economic Origins of US-China Strategic Competition", in Evan S. Medeiros, Ed., *Cold Rivals: The New Era of US-China Strategic Competition* (Washington, DC: Georgetown University Press), 2023, p. 172–204; Deborah Brautigam and Meg Rithmire, "The Chinese 'Debt Trap' Is a Myth", *The Atlantic*, February 6, 2021, www.theatlantic.com/international/archive/2021/02/china-debt-trap-diplomacy/617953/; Bates Gill, *Daring to Struggle: China's Global Ambitions under Xi Jinping* (New York: Oxford University Press), 2022, pp. 90–92;"Small Is Beautiful: A New Era in China's Overseas Development Finance?", BU Global Development Policy Center, Accessed July 12, 2023, www.bu.edu/gdp/2023/01/19/small-is-beautiful-a-new-era-in-chinas-overseas-development-finance/; Oyintarelado Moses, Cecilia Springer, and Kevin P. Gallagher, "Demystifying Chinese Overseas Lending and Development Finance: Why China Became the World's Largest Official Bilateral Lender", Boston University Global Development Policy Center, GCI Policy Brief 018, April 2023, www.bu.edu/gdp/files/2023/04/GCI_PB_018_Chinas_OLDF_FIN.pdf; Ann Scott-Tyson, "Is China Ensnaring Poor Countries by Building Their Infrastructure?", *The Christian Science Monitor*, December 20, 2021, www.csmonitor.com/World/Asia-Pacific/2021/1220/Is-China-ensnaring-poor-countries-by-building-their-infrastructure.

37 Xi Jinping, "Bolstering Confidence and Jointly Overcoming Difficulties to Build a Better World", statement by Xi Jinping at the General Debate of the 76th Session of the United Nations General Assembly, September 21, 2021, www.fmprc.gov.cn/mfa_eng/wjdt_665385/zyjh_665391/202109/t20210922_9580293.html; Deborah Brautigam, "The ABCs of China's GDI", *EastAsiaForum*, December 22, 2022, www.eastasiaforum.org/2022/12/22/the-abcs-of-chinas-gdi/.

38 "The Global Security Initiative Concept Paper" (China: Ministry of Foreign Affairs of the People's Republic of China), February 21, 2023, www.fmprc.gov.cn/mfa_eng/wjbxw/202302/t20230221_11028348.html.
39 Ibid.
40 "Joint Trilateral Statement by the People's Republic of China, the Kingdom of Saudi Arabia, and the Islamic Republic of Iran", Ministry of Foreign Affairs of the People's Republic of China, March 10, 2023, www.fmprc.gov.cn/eng/wjdt_665385/2649_665393/202303/t20230311_11039241.html; Mordechai Chaziza, "The Global Security Initiative: China's New Security Architecture for the Gulf", *The Diplomat*, May 5, 2023, https://thediplomat.com/2023/05/the-global-security-initiative-chinas-new-security-architecture-for-the-gulf/; David Pierson, "China's Role in Iran-Saudi Arabia Deal Shows Xi's Global Goals", *The New York Times*, March 11, 2023, www.nytimes.com/2023/03/11/world/asia/china-saudi-arabia-iran-us.html.
41 "Xi Jinping Attends the CPC in Dialogue with World Political Parties High-Level Meeting and Delivers a Keynote Speech", March 16, 2023, www.fmprc.gov.cn/eng/zxxx_662805/202303/t20230317_11043656.html.
42 "Chinese Modernization: New Opportunities for the World", Keynote Speech by H.E. State Council and Foreign Minister Qin Gang, at the Opening Ceremony of the Lanting Forum on Chinese modernization and the World", Shanghai, April 21, 2023, www.fmprc.gov.cn/eng/wjdt_665385/zyjh_665391/202304/t20230421_11062902.html.
43 Analysts have highlighted the possibility that China is "secretly selling [Russia] hi-tech products which could be used for military purposes" ("Ukraine War: What Support Is China Giving Russia", *BBC News*, March 20, 2023, www.bbc.com/news/60571253) but as of the time of this writing, there are no verified reports presenting concrete evidence to that effect. China also has taken advantage of the immediate opportunities made available by the West's sanctions regimes—cut-rate prices on Russian energy, for example—without overtly violating them. India, Turkey, and others have behaved similarly. See: Lizzi C. Lee, "China's Long Game in Russia: Violating Sanctions? No. Ensuring Russia's Survival? Yes". (Cambridge, MA: Harvard Kennedy School Belfer Center for Science and International Affairs), *Russia Matters*, June 30, 2022, www.russiamatters.org/analysis/chinas-long-game-russia-violating-sanctions-no-ensuring-russias-survival-yes; Felix K. Chang, "China's and India's Relations with Russia after the War in Ukraine: A Dangerous Deviation?" (Washington, DC: Foreign Policy Research Institute), April 5, 2023, www.fpri.org/article/2023/04/chinas-and-indias-relations-with-russia-after-the-war-in-ukraine-a-dangerous-deviation/; Mark Leonard, "What China Really Thinks about Ukraine", *Politico*, August 17, 2023, www.politico.eu/article/china-russia-ukraine-war-world-peace-forum/.

44 Daniel Victor, "Hong Kong Protests Put N.B.A. on Edge in China", *The New York Times*, October 7, 2019, www.nytimes. com/2019/10/07/sports/basketball/nba-china-hong-kong.html.

45 Victor Cha, "Examining China's Coercive Economic Tactics" (Testimony, U.S. House Committee on Rules), May 10, 2023, www.csis. org/analysis/examining-chinas-coercive-economic-tactics; Gerry Shih, "China Announces Sanctions against U.S.- Based Non-Profit Groups in Response to Congress's Hong Kong Legislation", *The Washington Post*, December 2, 2019, www.washingtonpost.com/world/asia-pacific/ china-announces-sanctions-against-us-based-nonprofits-in-response-to-congresss-hong-kong-legislation/2019/12/02/9f414616–14e0– 11ea-80d6-d0ca7007273f_story.html; Michelle Toh and Laura He, "All of the NBA's Official Chinese Partners Have Suspended Ties with the League", *CNN Business*, October 9, 2019, www.cnn.com/2019/10/09/ business/nba-china-partners/index.html.

46 Ralph Jennings, "How Vietnam Quietly Built Up 10 Islands in Asia's Most Disputed Sea", *Voice of America*, April 19, 2019, www. voanews.com/a/how-vietnam-quietly-built-up-10-islands-in-asia-most-disputed-sea/4882776.html.

47 Lawrence Chung, "10-Hour Stand-Off between Taiwanese Coastguard and Japanese Patrol Ship Sparks Call for Talks", *South China Morning Post*, October 5, 2022, www.scmp. com/news/china/diplomacy/article/3194916/10-hour-stand-between-taiwanese-coastguard-and-japanese-patrol; "Are Maritime Law Enforcement Forces Destabilizing Asia?", Washington, DC: CSIS, https://csis-ilab.github.io/cpower-viz/csis-china-sea/.

48 Sreenivasa Rao Pemmaraju, "The South China Sea Arbitration (The Philippines v. China): Assessment of the Award on Jurisdiction and Admissibility", *Chinese Journal of International Law*, Vol. 15, No. 2, June 2016, pp. 265–307, https://doi.org/10.1093/chinesejil/jmw019.

49 K. Parlett, "Jurisdiction of the Arbitral Tribunal in Philippines v. China under UNCLOS and in the Absence of China", *AJIL Unbound*, Vol. 110, 2016, pp. 266–272, https://doi.org/10.1017/ S2398772300009144; Ibid.

50 John Mueller, "The Case against Containment: The Strategy Didn't Win the Cold War—and it Won't Defeat China", *Foreign Affairs*, September 21, 2023, www.foreignaffairs.com/united-states/ case-against-containment.

51 Dmitry Dima Adamsky, "The 1983 Nuclear Crisis – Lessons for Deterrence Theory and Practice", *Journal of Strategic Studies*, Vol. 36, No. 1, 2013, pp. 4–41, https://doi.org/10.1080/01402390.2012.732015.

52 Michael Beckley, "Delusions of Detente: Why America and China Will Be Enduring Rivals", *Foreign Affairs*, August 22, 2023, www. foreignaffairs.com/united-states/china-delusions-detente-rivals.

53 Dame Meg Taylor DBE, "Pacific-Led Regionalism Undermined" (New York: Asia Society Policy Institute), September 2023, https:// asiasociety.org/policy-institute/pacific-led-regionalism-undermined.

54 Katy O'Donnell, "White House Rejects Democrats' Call for New IMF Emergency Reserves", *PoliticoPro*, October 5, 2023, https://subscriber.politicopro.com/article/2023/10/white-house-rejects-democrats-call-for-new-imf-emergency-reserves-00120177.

55 "Fact Sheet: Delivering a Better, Bigger, More Effective World Bank" (Washington, DC: The White House), September 9, 2023, www.whitehouse.gov/briefing-room/statements-releases/2023/09/09/fact-sheet-delivering-a-better-bigger-more-effective-world-bank/; "Fact Sheet: President Biden and G7 Leaders Formally Launch the Partnership for Global Infrastructure and Investment", 2022, www.whitehouse.gov/briefing-room/statements-releases/2022/06/26/fact-sheet-president-biden-and-g7-leaders-formally-launch-the-partnership-for-global-infrastructure-and-investment/.

56 Elbridge Colby and Jim Mitre, "Why the Pentagon Should Focus on Taiwan", *War on the Rocks*, October 7, 2020, https://warontherocks.com/2020/10/why-the-pentagon-should-focus-on-taiwan/; Jennifer Lind, "Life in China's Asia: What Regional Hegemony Would Look Like", *Foreign Affairs*, March/April 2018, www.foreignaffairs.com/articles/china/2018-02-13/life-chinas-asia; John Feng, "China Invasion of Taiwan Would Threaten US Credibility in Asia, Top Admiral Warns", *Newsweek*, March 24, 2021; Richard Haass and David Sacks, "The Growing Danger of U.S. Ambiguity on Taiwan", *Foreign Affairs*, December 13, 2021, www.foreignaffairs.com/articles/china/2021-12-13/growing-danger-us-ambiguity-taiwan.

57 Long-term and well-respected defense experts David Ochmanek and Andrew Hoehn have been unequivocal about the fact that "much of [U.S. military] superiority is gone—surely with respect to China but in significant ways with respect to the forces of other, less powerful adversaries as well—and it is not coming back". David Ochmanek and Andrew Hoehn, "Inflection Point: How to Reverse the Erosion of U.S. and Allied Military Power and Influence", *War on the Rocks*, November 3, 2023, https://warontherocks.com/2023/11/inflection-point-how-to-reverse-the-erosion-of-u-s-and-allied-military-power-and-influence/.

58 Michael E. O'Hanlon, "Can China Take Taiwan? Why No One Really Knows" (Washington, DC: The Brookings Institution), August 2022, www.brookings.edu/articles/can-china-take-taiwan-why-no-one-really-knows/.

59 Melanie W. Sisson, "Taiwan and the Dangerous Illogic of Deterrence by Denial" (Washington, DC: The Brookings Institution), May 2022, www.brookings.edu/articles/taiwan-and-the-dangerous-illogic-of-deterrence-by-denial/.

60 "New Guidelines for U.S. Government Interactions with Taiwan Counterparts", press statement of Ned Price, Department spokesperson, April 9, 2021, www.state.gov/new-guidelines-for-u-s-government-interactions-with-taiwan-counterparts/; Chao Deng and Chun Han Wong, "Biden Sends Important Foreign-Policy Signal with Taiwan Inauguration Invite", *The Wall Street Journal*, January 21, 2021,

www.wsj.com/articles/biden-sends-important-foreign-policy-signal-with-taiwan-inauguration-invite-11611230623; "Participant List: Summit for Democracy", U.S. Department of State, 2021, www.state.gov/participant-list-the-summit-for-democracy/.

61 Russell Hsiao, "Senior US Defense Official Reaffirms Reagan's Assurances to Taiwan", *Global Taiwan Institute*, Vol. 3, No. 15, July 25, 2018, https://globaltaiwan.org/2018/07/vol-3-issue-15/#RussellHsiao07252018.

62 Erin Hale, "US Nearly Doubled Military Personnel Stationed in Taiwan this Year", *VOA News*, December 2, 2021, www.voanews.com/a/pentagon-us-nearly-doubled-military-personnel-stationed-in-taiwan-this-year-/6337695.html; "China Urges U.S. to Abide by Deal to Keep Troops Out of Taiwan", *Bloomberg News*, October 8, 2021, www.bloomberg.com/news/articles/2021-10-08/china-calls-on-u-s-to-withdraw-american-troops-from-taiwan.

63 "Timeline: U.S. Arms Sales to Taiwan in 2020 Total $5 Billion Amid China Tensions", *Reuters*, December 7, 2020, www.reuters.com/article/us-taiwan-security-usa-timeline/timeline-u-s-arms-sales-to-taiwan-in-2020-total-5-billion-amid-china-tensions-idUSKBN28I0BF; Joseph Choi, "Lawmakers Call for End to 'Strategic Ambiguity' on Taiwan", *The Hill*, October 7, 2021, https://thehill.com/policy/defense/575842-lawmakers-call-for-end-to-strategic-ambiguity-on-taiwan; Richard Haass and David Sacks, "The Growing Danger of U.S. Ambiguity on Taiwan".

64 Keith B. Richburg, "China Fires 3 Missiles into Sea Near Taiwan", *The Washington Post*, March 18, 1996, www.washingtonpost.com/archive/politics/1996/03/08/china-fires-3-missiles-into-sea-near-taiwan/bf5aa0eb-6078-4b3b-a0b6-fc547ef36127/; Akit Panda, "Taipei Slams 'Provocative' Chinese Air Force Fighters Cross Taiwan Strait Median Line", *The Diplomat*, April 1, 2019, https://thediplomat.com/2019/04/taipei-slams-provocative-chinese-air-force-fighters-cross-taiwan-strait-median-line/; Ben Blanchard and Yew Lun Tian, "Taiwan Scrambles Jets as 18 Chinese Planes Buzz during U.S. Visit", *Reuters*, September 17, 2020, www.reuters.com/article/us-taiwan-usa-china/taiwan-scrambles-jets-as-18-chinese-planes-buzz-during-u-s-visit-idUSKBN2690AS; Ben Blanchard and Yimou Lee, "China Mounts Largest Incursion Yet near Taiwan, Blames U.S. for Tensions", *Reuters*, October 4, 2021, www.reuters.com/world/asia-pacific/taiwan-reports-surge-chinese-aircraft-defence-zone-2021-10-04/; Huizhong Wu, "China Sends 39 Warplanes toward Taiwan, Largest in New Year", *Military Times*, January 24, 2022, www.militarytimes.com/flashpoints/2022/01/24/china-sends-39-warplanes-toward-taiwan-largest-in-new-year/?utm_source=Sailthru&utm_medium=email&utm_campaign=EBB%2001.24.2022&utm_term=Editorial%20-%20Early%20Bird%20Brief; Lily Kuo, "China's Military Extends Drills near Taiwan after Pelosi Trip", *The Washington Post*, August 8, 2022, www.washingtonpost.com/world/2022/08/08/taiwan-china-military-exercises-pelosi/.

65 Allen Carlson, *Unifying China, Integrating with the World: Securing Chinese Sovereignty in the Reform Era* (Stanford, CA: Stanford University Press), 2005, p. 36.

66 Zhiguo Gao and Bing Bing Jia, "The Nine-Dash Line in the South China Sea: History, Status, and Implications", *The American Journal of International Law*, Vol. 107, No. 1, 2013, pp. 98–124, www.jstor.org/stable/10.5305/amerjintelaw.107.1.0098; Gregory B. Poling, *On Dangerous Ground: America's Century in the South China Sea* (New York: Oxford University Press), 2022, pp. 17–18, 30–31; Alec Caruana, "Maritime Affairs Program (MAP) Handbill Spotlight: Nine-Dash Line" (Washington, DC: The Institute for China-America Studies), July 25, 2023, https://chinaus-icas.org/research/map-spotlight-nine-dash-line/; Douglas J. Verblaauw, "Degrading China's Integrated Maritime Campaign", *Joint Force Quarterly*, Vol. 103, October 14, 2021, pp. 54–61, https://ndu-press.ndu.edu/Media/News/News-Article-View/Article/2808063/degrading-chinas-integrated-maritime-campaign/.

67 Zhiguo Gao and Bing Bing Jia, "The Nine-Dash Line in the South China Sea: History, Status, and Implications", 2013.

68 Kun-Chin Lin and Andres Villar Gertner, "Maritime Security in the Asia-Pacific: China and the Emerging Order in the East and South China Seas" (London: Chatham House), July 2015, p. 23, www.chathamhouse.org/sites/default/files/CHHJ3432_Maritime_Research_paper_07.15_WEB_14.08.15.pdf.

69 "Remarks by Antony J. Blinken, Secretary of State, U.S. Embassy Annex, Hanoi, Vietnam", April 15, 2023, www.state.gov/secretary-antony-j-blinken-at-a-press-availability-33/.

70 China, in fact, seems to be pursuing a similar strategy by allowing, enabling, or perhaps directing paramilitary actors to become increasingly aggressive in their tactics in its near seas while, at the same time, seeking to reinvigorate discussion among the countries of the Association of Southeast Asian Nations (ASEAN) on a binding code of conduct (CoC) on the South China Sea. See: Chris Lau, Jennifer Hauser, and Chloe Liu, "China and Philippines Accuse Each Other over Collisions in Disputed South China Sea", *CNN*, October 23, 2023, www.cnn.com/2023/10/22/asia/south-china-sea-philippines-collision-intl-hnk/index.html; Prashanth Parameswaran, "What's Behind the New China-ASEAN South China Sea Code of Conduct Talk Guidelines?" (Washington, DC: The Wilson Center), *Asia Dispatches*, July 25, 2023, www.wilsoncenter.org/blog-post/whats-behind-new-china-asean-south-china-sea-code-conduct-talk-guidelines.

71 Melanie W. Sisson and Dan Patt, "A Deterrence Response Monitoring Capability for the U.S. Department of Defense" (Washington, DC: The Brookings Institution), June, 2023, www.brookings.edu/articles/a-deterrence-response-monitoring-capability-for-the-us-department-of-defense/.

72 M. Taylor Fravel, "Regime Insecurity and International Cooperation: Explaining China's Compromises in Territorial Disputes",
International Security, Vol. 30, No. 2, 2005, pp. 46–83, www.jstor.
org/stable/4137595.
73 "Military and Security Developments Involving the People's republic of China" (Washington, DC: U.S. Department of Defense),
2023, p. 154, https://media.defense.gov/2023/Oct/19/2003323409
/-1/-1/1/2023-MILITARY-AND-SECURITY-DEVELOPMENTS-IN
VOLVING-THE-PEOPLES-REPUBLIC-OF-CHINA.PDF.
74 Isaac Kardon and Jennifer Kavanagh, "China Is Trying to Have It
Both Ways in the Middle East", *The New York Times*, January 26,
2024, www.nytimes.com/2024/01/26/opinion/china-redsea-houthi-
shipping.html.
75 Mallory Shelbourne, "Pentagon Officials Provide Data on Unsafe Chi
nese Fighter Intercepts over Western Pacific", *USNI News*, October 17,
2023, https://news.usni.org/2023/10/17/pentagon-officials-provid
e-data-on-unsafe-chinese-fighter-intercepts-over-western-pacific.
76 Lily Kuo, "The Next Front in the Tech War with China: Graphite (and
Clean Energy)", *The Washington Post*, November 29, 2023, www.
washingtonpost.com/world/2023/11/29/china-critical-minerals-
graphite-trade-united-states/.
77 Ryan Hass, *Stronger: Adapting America's China Strategy in an Age
of Competitive Interdependence* (New Haven, CT: Yale University
Press), 2021.

ADDITIONAL SOURCES CONSULTED

Alastair Iain Johnston, *Chinese Strategic Culture and the Parabellum Paradigm* (Princeton, NJ: Princeton University Press), 1995.

Alastair Iain Johnston, "China in a World of Orders: Rethinking Compliance and Challenge in Beijing's International Relations", *International Security*, Vol. 44, No. 2, 2019, pp. 9–60, https://doi.org/10.1162/isec_a_00360.

Andrew J. Nathan, "China's Rise and International Regimes: Does China Seek to Overthrow Global Norms?", in Robert S. Ross and Jo Inge Bekkevold, Eds., *China in the Era of Xi Jinping: Domestic and Foreign Policy Challenges* (Washington, DC: Georgetown University Press), 2016, pp. 165–195, http://www.jstor.org/stable/j.ctt1c2crg2.11.

Andrew J. Nathan, "The New Tiananmen Papers: Inside the Secret Meeting that Changed China", *Foreign Affairs*, July/August 2019, https://www.foreignaffairs.com/articles/china/2019-05-30/new-tiananmen-papers.

Andrew J. Nathan, "The Tiananmen Papers", *Foreign Affairs*, January/February 2001, https://www.foreignaffairs.com/articles/asia/2001-01-01/tiananmen-papers.

Andrew Small, *No Limits: The Inside Story of China's War with the West* (London: Melville House), 2022.

Annabelle Timsit, "When the World Outlawed War", *The Atlantic*, October 19, 2017, https://www.theatlantic.com/international/archive/2017/10/the-internationalists-war-peace-oona-hathaway-scott-shapiro/542550/.

Anne-Marie Slaughter, "Security, Solidarity, and Sovereignty: The Grand Themes of UN Reform", *The American Journal of International Law*, Vol. 99, No. 3, 2005, pp. 619–631, https://doi.org/10.2307/1602294.

Athan Theoharis, "Roosevelt and Truman on Yalta: The Origins of the Cold War", *Political Science Quarterly*, Vol. 87, No. 2, 1972, pp. 210–241, https://doi.org/10.2307/2147826.

Ban Wang, Ed., *Chinese Visions of World Order: Tianxia, Culture, and World Politics* (Durham, NC: Duke University Press), 2017.

Bates Gill, "Contrasting Visions: United States, China and World Order: Remarks Presented Before the U.S.-China Security Review Commission

Session on U.S.-China Relationship and Strategic Perceptions" (Washington, DC: The Brookings Institution), August 3, 2001, https://www.brookings.edu/wp-content/uploads/2016/06/20010803-1.pdf.

Bates Gill, *Daring to Struggle: China's Global Ambitions under Xi Jinping* (New York: Oxford University Press), 2022.

Bereket Habte Selassie, "The World Bank: Power and Responsibility in Historical Perspective", *African Studies Review*, Vol. 27, No. 4, 1984, pp. 35–46, https://doi.org/10.2307/524056.

Bruce Jones and Andrew Yeo, "China and the Challenge to Global Order" (Washington, DC: The Brookings Institution), November2022,https://www.brookings.edu/articles/china-and-the-challenge-to-global-order/.

Byron S. Weng, "Communist China's Changing Attitudes toward the United Nations", *International Organization*, Vol. 20, No. 4, 1966, pp. 677–704, http://www.jstor.org/stable/2705736.

C. Pearson, "Stability and Instability in the International Monetary System", *IFAC Proceedings Volumes*, Vol. 16, No. 17, 1983, pp. 43–53.

Charles A. Kupchan, *Isolationism: A History of America's Efforts to Shield Itself from the World* (New York: Oxford University Press), 2020.

Charles S. Maier, "The Politics of Productivity: Foundations of American International Economic Policy After World War II", *International Organization*, Vol. 31, No. 4, 1977, pp. 607–633, http://www.jstor.org/stable/2706316.

Charlotte Ku, "Abolition of China's Unequal Treaties and the Search for Regional Stability in Asia, 1919–1943", *Texas A&M Law Scholarship*, Vol. 1, 1994, pp. 67–86, https://scholarship.law.tamu.edu/cgi/viewcontent.cgi?referer=https://www.google.com/&httpsredir=1&article=1412&context=facscholar.

Cristina L. Garafola, Stephen Watts, and Kristin J. Leuschner, "China's Global Basing Ambitions: Defense Implications for the United States" (Santa Monica, CA: RAND Corporation), 2022, https://www.rand.org/pubs/research_reports/RRA1496-1.html.

Daniel Drezner, "Is There an Exceptional American Approach to Global Economic Governance?", in G. John Ikenberry, Wang Jisi, and Zhu Feng, Eds., *America, China, and the Struggle for World Order: Ideas, Traditions, Historical Legacies, and Global Visions* (New York: Palgrave MacMillan), 2015, Chapter 5, pp. 135–160.

David A. Kay, "The United Nations and United States Foreign Policy", *Proceedings of the Academy of Political Science*, Vol. 32, No. 4, 1977, pp. 11–16, https://doi.org/10.2307/1173987.

David M. Lampton, "China and Clinton's America: Have They Learned Anything?", *Asian Survey*, Vol. 37, No. 12, December 1997, pp. 1099–1118, https://www.jstor.org/stable/2645760.

Edward T. Rowe, "The United States, the United Nations, and the Cold War", *International Organization*, Vol. 25, No. 1, 1971, pp. 59–78, http://www.jstor.org/stable/2705980.

Elbridge Colby, *The Strategy of Denial: American Defense in an Age of Great Power Conflict* (New Haven, CT: Yale University Press), 2021.

Elizabeth C. Economy, *The World According to China* (Medford: Polity Press), 2022.

Fareed Zakaria, "The Reagan Strategy of Containment", *Political Science Quarterly*, Vol. 105, No. 3, 1990, pp. 373–395.

Fiona S. Cunningham, "The Unknowns about China's Nuclear Modernization Program" (Washington, DC: Arms Control Association), June 2023, https://www.armscontrol.org/act/2023-06/features/unknowns-about-chinas-nuclear-modernization-program.

Francine McKenzie, "GATT and the Cold War: Accession Debates, Institutional Development, and the Western Alliance, 1947–1959", *Journal of Cold War Studies*, Vol. 10, No. 3, 2008, pp. 78–109, https://www.jstor.org/stable/26922776.

Francine McKenzie, "Peace, Prosperity and Planning Postwar Trade, 1942–1948", in Michel Christian, Sandrine Kott, and Ondřej Matějka, Eds., *Planning in Cold War Europe: Competition, Cooperation, Circulations (1950s–1970s)* (Berlin/Boston, MA: De Gruyter), 2018, 1st ed., pp. 21–44, http://www.jstor.org/stable/j.ctvbkjvbs.4.

Francis J. Gavin, "Asking the Right Questions About the Past and Future of World Order", *War on the Rocks*, January 20, 2020, https://warontherocks.com/2020/01/asking-the-right-questions-about-the-past-and-future-of-world-order/

G. John Ikenberry, *After Victory: Institutions, Strategic Restraint, and the Rebuilding of Order after Major Wars* (Princeton, NJ: Princeton University Press), 2001.

G. John Ikenberry, "Why American Power Endures: The U.S.-Led Order Isn't in Decline", *Foreign Affairs*, Vol. 101, No. 6, November/December 2022, pp. 56–73.

G. John Ikenberry and Daniel Deudney, "The Nature and Sources of Liberal International Order", *Review of International Studies*, Vol. 25, No. 2, 1999, pp. 179–196.

G. John Ikenberry, Wang Jisi, and Zhu Feng, Eds., *America, China, and the Struggle for World Order: Ideas, Traditions, Historical Legacies, and Global Visions* (New York: Palgrave Macmillan), 2015.

Gabriele Wight and Brian Porter, Eds., *International Theory: The Three Traditions* (New York: Holmes & Meier), 1992.

Gavin Bade, " 'A Sea Change': Biden Reverses Decades of Chinese Trade Policy", *Politico*, December 26, 2022.

Gavin Bade, "Joe Biden Wants a 'New Economic World Order.' It's Never Looked More Disordered", *Politico*, May 25, 2023, https://www.politico.com/news/2023/05/25/joe-bidens-economy-trade-china-00096781.

Gideon Rachman, "Is There Such a Thing as a Rules-Based International Order?", *The Financial Times*, April 20, 2023, https://www.ft.com/content/664d7fa5-d575-45da-8129-095647c8abe7.

Hal Brands, "American Grand Strategy and the Liberal Order: Continuity, Change, and Options for the Future" (Santa Monica, CA: RAND), 2016.

Hedley Bull, *The Anarchical Society: A Study of Order in World Politics* (New York: Columbia University Press), 1977.

Henry Kissinger, *World Order* (New York: Penguin Books), 2015.

Herbert Butterfield and Martin Wight, *Diplomatic Investigations: Essays in the Theory of International Politics* (Cambridge, MA: Harvard University Press), 1966.

Inis L. Claude, "The United Nations, the United States, and the Maintenance of Peace", *International Organization*, Vol. 23, No. 3, 1969, pp. 621–636, http://www.jstor.org/stable/2706073.

Isaac B. Kardon, *China's Law of the Sea: The New Rules of Maritime Order* (New Haven, CT: Yale University Press), 2023.

Jeffrey Feltman, "China's Expanding Influence at the United Nations— and How the United States Should React" (Washington, DC: The Brookings Institution), September 2020, https://www.brookings.edu/wp-content/uploads/2020/09/FP_20200914_china_united_nations_feltman.pdf.

Jeffrey W. Legro, *Rethinking the World: Great Power Strategies and International Order* (Ithaca, NY: Cornell University Press), 2005.

Jeffrey W. Legro, "What China Will Want: The Future Intentions of a Rising Power", *Perspectives on Politics*, Vol. 5, No. 3, 2007, pp. 515–534.

Joel J. Kupperman, *Learning from Asian Philosophy* (New York: Oxford University Press), 1999.

Joel Wuthnow, "China and the Processes of Cooperation in UN Security Council Deliberations", *The Chinese Journal of International Politics*, Vol. 3, No. 1, 2010, pp. 55–77, https://www.jstor.org/stable/48615780.

John Bew, "World Order: Many-Headed Monster or Noble Pursuit?", *Texas National Security Review*, Vol. 1, No. 1, November 2017, pp. 14–35, https://tnsr.org/2017/11/world-order-many-headed-monster-noble-pursuit/.

John Gerard Ruggie, "International Regimes, Transactions, and Change: Embedded Liberalism in the Postwar Economic Order", *International Organization*, Vol. 36, No. 2, 1982, pp. 379–415.

John Gerard Ruggie, "The United States and the United Nations: Toward a New Realism", *International Organization*, Vol. 39, No. 2, Spring 1985, pp. 343–356, https://www.jstor.org/stable/2706713.

John King Fairbank, Ed., *The Chinese World Order: Traditional China's Foreign Relations* (Cambridge, MA: Harvard University Press), 1968.

John Trent and Laura Schnurr, "Promoting and Protecting Human Rights", in John Trent and Laura Schnurr, Eds., *A United Nations Renaissance: What the UN Is, and What it Could Be* (Leverkusen: Verlag Barbara Budrich), 2018, 1st ed., pp. 98–123, https://doi.org/10.2307/j.ctvdf03xp.9.

Judith L. Goldstein, Douglas Rivers, and Michael Tomz, "Institutions in International Relations: Understanding the Effects of the GATT and the WTO on World Trade", *International Organization*, Vol. 61, No. 1, 2007, pp. 37–67, http://www.jstor.org/stable/4498137.

Kenneth Waltz, *Theory of International Politics* (New York: McGraw-Hill), 1979.

Kerry Dumbaugh, "China-U.S. Relations: Chronology of Developments During the Clinton Administration", *CRS Report for Congress* (Washington, DC: Congressional Research Service), July 25, 2000.

Keyu Jin, *The New China Playbook: Beyond Socialism and Capitalism* (New York: Viking), 2023.

Larry Blomstedt, "Into Korea", in Larry Blomstedt, *Truman, Congress, and Korea: The Politics of America's First Undeclared War* (Lexington, KY: University Press of Kentucky), 2016, pp. 23–54, https://doi.org/10.2307/j.ctt189ttn6.5.

Lee (李賢中), H. Lee, "Considering the Present from the Past: On Mohist Thought and its Modern Transformation", *Journal of Chinese Humanities*, Vol. 7, Nos. 1–2, 2021, pp. 79–111, https://doi.org/10.1163/23521341-12340109.

Leland M. Goodrich, "The United Nations and the Korean War: A Case Study", *Proceedings of the Academy of Political Science*, Vol. 25, No. 2, 1953, pp. 90–104, https://doi.org/10.2307/1173269.

Liza Tobin, "Xi's Vision for Transforming Global Governance: A Strategic Challenge for Washington and its Allies", *Texas National Security Review*, Vol. 2, No. 1, November 2018, pp. 154–166, http://doi.org/10.26153/tsw/863.

M. A. Fitzsimons, "The Suez Crisis and the Containment Policy", *The Review of Politics*, Vol. 19, No. 4, October 1957, pp. 419–445.

Marc Trachtenberg, "The Berlin Crisis", in Marc Trachtenberg, *History and Strategy* (Princeton, NJ: Princeton University Press), 1991, pp. 169–234, https://doi.org/10.2307/j.ctv14163z4.8.

Marc Trachtenberg, "The Problem of International Order and How to Think About it", *The Monist*, Vol. 89, No. 2, April 2006, pp. 207–231.

Martin Jacques, *When China Rules the World: The End of the Western World and the Birth of a New Global Order* (New York: Penguin), 2012.

Michael A. Peters, "The Chinese Dream: Xi Jinping Thought on Socialism with Chinese Characteristics for a New Era", *Educational Philosophy and Theory*, Vol. 49, No. 14, 2017, pp. 1299–1304, https://doi.org/10.1080/00131857.2017.1407578.

Michael Doyle, *Cold Peace: Avoiding the New Cold War* (New York: W.W. Norton & Company), 2023.

Michael J. Mazarr et al., "Understanding the Current International Order" (Santa Monica, CA: RAND), 2016, https://www.rand.org/pubs/research_reports/RR1598.html.

Michael Pillsbury, *The Hundred Year Marathon: China's Secret Strategy to Replace America as the Global Superpower* (New York: Henry Holt & Company LLC), 2015.

Michael Schuman, *Superpower Interrupted: The Chinese History of the World* (New York: Hachette Book Group), 2020.

Minxin Pei, "International Development Cooperation in the Age of US-China Strategic Rivalry" (Washington, DC: Brookings Institution), July 25, 2019, https://www.brookings.edu/articles/international-development-cooperation-in-the-age-of-us-china-strategic-rivalry/.

Orville Schell and John Delury, *Wealth and Power: China's Long March to the Twenty-First Century* (New York: Random House), 2014.

Pan Zhenquiang, "China's No First Use of Nuclear Weapons", in Li Bin and Tong Zhao, Eds., *Understanding Chinese Nuclear Thinking* (Washington, DC: Carnegie Endowment for International Peace), 2016, pp. 51–77, http://www.jstor.org/stable/resrep26903.7.

Penelope B. Prime, "China Joins the WTO: How, Why and What Now?", *Business Economics*, Vol. XXXVII, No. 2, 2002, pp. 26–32.

Peter Drysdale and Samuel Hardwick, "China and the Global Trading System: Then and Now", in Ross Garnaut, Ligang Song, and Cai Fang, Eds., *China's 40 Years of Reform and Development: 1978–2018* (Canberra: ANU Press), 2018, pp. 545–574, http://www.jstor.org/stable/j.ctv5cgbnk.35.

Philip C. Jessup, "The Berlin Blockade and the Use of the United Nations", *Foreign Affairs*, October 1971.

Rebecca Lissner and Mira Rapp-Hooper, *An Open World: How America Can Win the Contest for Twenty-First-Century Order* (New Haven, CT: Yale University Press), 2020.

Richard N. Gardner, "The Soviet Union and the United Nations", *Law and Contemporary Problems*, Vol. 29, No. 4, 1964, pp. 845–857, https://doi.org/10.2307/1190697.

Richard N. Swift, "United States Leadership in the United Nations", *The Western Political Quarterly*, Vol. 11, No. 2, 1958, pp. 183–194, https://doi.org/10.2307/444400.

Richard Toye, "Developing Multilateralism: The Havana Charter and the Fight for the International Trade Organization, 1947–48", *The International History Review*, Vol. 25, No. 2, June 2003, p. 282.

Robert Kagan, *Dangerous Nation* (New York: Alfred A. Knopf), 2006.

Robert Kagan, "War and the Liberal Hegemony", *Liberties*, Vol. 2, No. 4, 2022.

Robert L. Messer, "Paths not Taken: The United States Department of State and Alternatives to Containment, 1945–1946", *Diplomatic History*, Vol. 1, No. 4, Fall 1977, pp. 297–319.

Robert Pee and William Michael Schmidli, Eds., *The Reagan Administration, the Cold War, and the Transition to Democracy Promotion* (Cham: Palgrave Macmillan), 2019.

Ross N. Berkes, "The United Nations and the Cold War Conflict", *Current History*, Vol. 37, No. 218, 1959, pp. 228–238, http://www.jstor.org/stable/45310332.

Rudd, Kevin, *The Avoidable War: The Dangers of a Catastrophic Conflict between the US and Xi Jinping's China* (New York: Hachette Book Group, Inc.), 2022.

Russell H. Fifield, "The Five Principles of Peaceful Co-Existence", *The American Journal of International Law*, Vol. 52, No. 3, July 1958, pp. 5014–5510, https://www.jstor.org/stable/2195465.

Samuel P. Huntington, "Political Development and Political Decay", *World Politics*, Vol. 17, No. 3, April 1965, pp. 386–430: https://www.jstor.org/stable/pdf/2009286.pdf?casa_token=SfiXo13VZYM AAAAA:sFA4SJKHeBcidNpXOWTK-fbOqZ-s030viqxWh78AwoO uemQR9r26uuhsb08um2g7r-SkMDqhLfOliWPtAWYk2thAZ2Lwc 8DG2ZWJ9KaClQinEEZAksKn.

Samuel S. Kim, *China, the United Nations and World Order* (Princeton, NJ: Princeton University Press), 1979.

Shaohua Hu, "Confucianism and Contemporary Chinese Politics", *Politics & Policy*, Vol. 35, No. 1, March 2007, pp. 1–163.

Stephen D. Krasner, "Sovereignty", *Foreign Policy*, No. 122, 2001, pp. 20–29, https://doi.org/10.2307/3183223.

Stephen Roach, *Accidental Conflict; America, China, and the Clash of False Narratives* (London: Yale University Press), 2022.

Suisheng Zhao, *The Dragon Roars Back: Transformational Leaders and Dynamics of Chinese Foreign Policy* (Stanford, CA: Stanford University Press), 2023.

Thomas F. Lynch III, James Przystup, and Phillip C. Saunders, "The Indo-Pacific Competitive Space: China's Vision and the Post–World War II American Order" (Washington, DC: National Defense University Press), November 4, 2020, https://ndupress.ndu.edu/Media/News/News-Article-View/Article/2404551/9-the-indo-pacific-competitive-space-chinas-vision-and-the-postworld-war-ii-ame/.

Vincent P. de Santis, "Eisenhower Revisionism", *The Review of Politics*, Vol. 38, No. 2, 1976, pp. 190–207, http://www.jstor.org/stable/1405936.

William A. Callahan, "Chinese Visions of World Order: Post-Hegemonic or a New Hegemony?", *International Studies Review*, Vol. 10, No. 4, 2008, pp. 749–761.

Yael S. Aronoff, "In like a Lamb, out like a Lion: The Political Conversion of Jimmy Carter", *Political Science Quarterly*, Vol. 121, No. 3, 2006, pp. 425–449, http://www.jstor.org/stable/20202726.

Yan Xuetong, "Becoming Strong: The New Chinese Foreign Policy", *Foreign Policy*, June 22, 2021, https://www.foreignaffairs.com/articles/united-states/2021-06-22/becoming-strong.

Yong Deng, "Hegemon on the Offensive: Chinese Perspectives on U. S. Global Strategy", *Political Science Quarterly*, Vol. 116, No. 3, 2001, pp. 343–365, https://doi.org/10.2307/798020.

Yongjin Zhang, "The Idea of Order in Ancient Chinese Political Thought: A Wightian Exploration", *International Affairs*, Vol. 90, No. 1, 2014, pp. 167–183, https://ciaotest.cc.columbia.edu/journals/riia/v90i1/f_0029985_24267.pdf.

Yue Hou, "The Evolving Relationship between the Party and the Private Sector in the Xi Era", in Jacques de Lisle and Guobin Yang, Eds., *The Party Leads All: The Evolving Role of the Chinese Communist Party* (Washington, DC: Brookings Institution Press), 2022.

Zheng Wang, "National Humiliation, History Education, and the Politics of Historical Memory: Patriotic Education Campaign in China", *International Studies Quarterly*, Vol. 52, No. 4, December 2008, pp. 783–806.

Zuo Fengrong, "A Review of Chinese Scholarship on the Collapse of the Soviet Union", Interpret: China (Washington, DC: CSIS), translation from Issues of Contemporary *World Socialism*, February 5, 2022, https://interpret.csis.org/translations/a-review-of-chinese-scholarship-on-the-collapse-of-the-soviet-union/.

INDEX

Printed in the United States
by Baker & Taylor Publisher Services